COLUMBUS
PIZZA

COLUMBUS PIZZA

A SLICE OF HISTORY

JIM ELLISON

THE
History
PRESS

Published by American Palate
A Division of The History Press
Charleston, SC
www.historypress.com

All photos from author's collection, unless otherwise noted.

First published 2020

Manufactured in the United States

ISBN 9781467143769

Library of Congress Control Number: 2020944527

Notice: The information in this book is true and complete to the best of our knowledge. It is offered without guarantee on the part of the author or The History Press. The author and The History Press disclaim all liability in connection with the use of this book.

CONTENTS

Foreword   7
Acknowledgements   9
Introduction   11

1. Primordial Pizza   15
2. Pioneers of Columbus Pizza (1950–54)   21
3. Pillars of Pizza   35
4. Pizza Proliferates (1955–69)   45
5. Pizza Preeminence (1970–84)   69
6. Pizza Peaks (1985–99)   89
7. Pizza Permutations (2000–20)   109
8. The Future of Pizza in Columbus   137

Bibliography   143
About the Author   159

FOREWORD

t a time when many mom-and-pop restaurants have fallen by the wayside in favor of national chains, author Jim Ellison takes us on a journey through the history and foundation of all the great pizza shops to ever call central Ohio home. What follows is a meticulously researched look back on how several industrious immigrant families, many from the same region in Italy, began, in mid-twentieth-century America, to create a new style of pizza all their own. Their efforts have, in large part, made Columbus, Ohio, the standard bearer and test market for American-style pizza. While other larger cities rightly claim specific styles of pizza their own, such as Chicago, New York and Detroit, Columbus has been recognized for decades as the home of classic pizza in the country.

Jim brings real enthusiasm and attention to detail throughout many interconnected tales, as told by the descendants of the founding families. Through serious research and dozens of interviews, he has stitched together a family tree of Columbus pizza, with stories of fathers, mothers, sons and daughters, who despite being competitors, created a mutual support system in the mostly Italian community. The book begins by connecting the dots, tracing the development of Columbus pizza from the earliest days in an area known then as Flytown, just south of today's Victorian Village, successively to Franklinton, Italian Village, Grandview and Arlington, with a few outliers on the East and South sides. From there, he explores techniques and inventions and recipes that originated in Columbus and went on to be adopted by the industry on a national level.

More than anything, this book harkens back to an earlier, less corporate time, when families still worked shoulder to shoulder in shop, often from a very young age. It transports us back to a time before economies of scale allowed large regional and national chains to eclipse the smaller shops and neighborhood favorites. As we venture further down this new path, this compendium of tales reminds us of the value of local purveyors. This book should encourage all to support and cherish them through our patronage.

—Richard G. Terapak, WOSU Chefs in the City
—Richard B. Terapak, WOSU Chefs in the City

ACKNOWLEDGEMENTS

There are too many people to list to thank everyone for their help with this book. And there are a few who cannot be thanked enough. First and foremost, my wife, Jamie. I dedicate this book to her.

Father Massuci, who returned an odd (maybe desperate) call from a kid who went to Watterson when the father was a hardcore Hartley devotee. The insights and information he provided on his father, Jimmy Massey, were incredibly helpful. Laura Sirij was a great source of information on Romeo's and her father, Romeo Sirij. It turns out that I went to high school with two of her sons. She lived in a house that I had passed by thousands of times in my lifetime. It was also impressive to find someone who even I thought was a zealot about Columbus Pizza history. The DiPaolo and Mizer families from RDP have been huge cheerleaders and were generous with their time and knowledge. The "Baldini Brothers," Ray Eal and Nick Ray, at RDP are my idols and helped connect some dots when needed. Jimmy Corrova at TAT was gracious with his time and fed me well. A big thank you to The History Press editor John Rodrigue for his patience and enthusiasm as this one-year project became a bit of an odyssey and took much longer than expected. When I had some unplanned free time to crank out the manuscript in early 2020, he helped me get the book rolling ahead of my much-revised schedule. Last but not least, thank you for buying this book.

On a final note, a disclaimer. Memories can be faulty or selective, and the record-keeping of businesses and information about them prior to 1970 is spotty at best. On occasion, if I was presented with conflicting memories of key events in Columbus Pizza history, I went with the most probable story. If I missed something important to you or our history, I apologize.

If you want to share your story about pizza, send an email to
ColumbusPizzaHistory@gmail.com.
Or connect with us on Instagram to see what is new
@CbusPizzaHistory

INTRODUCTION

Does Columbus have an iconic food? The initial answer is typically no. As has been the nature of Columbus residents for generations, the next impulse is to think of "big cities" and compare what they have to offer in contrast to our city. There are many foods synonymous with American cities: Philadelphia cheesesteaks, Buffalo wings, Seattle coffee, Boston clam chowder, New Orleans beignets, Baltimore crab cakes and so many more. Pizza in the form of highly defined styles is intertwined with the identities of Chicago, New York, New Haven, Detroit and a handful of other cities. Add to that list Columbus. There is no food that is more infused in the character of our city than pizza. Over the course of a century, it has become a definitive American food, and since the 1950s, Columbus pizza has had a national influence on an expanding pizza industry while pleasing our palates and feeding the families in our fair city.

The first pizza in Columbus was served at the original Flytown location of TAT Ristorante as early as 1934. This ties TAT with what some have listed as the first pizzeria in the state, Pizzi Café in Conneaut. The first pizzeria in Columbus was Romeo's, which opened in December 1950. The early tagline in its ads was "1950, the year Columbus discovered Pizza." The growth of pizza in Columbus from the 1950s to the beginning of the twenty-first century would best be described as meteoric. Along the way, a very specific style of pizza developed here, starting in the mid-1950s and continuing to this day, guided by the experiences and culinary interpretations of a handful of people, including Jimmy Massey, Romeo

Sirij, Tommy Iacono, Joe Gatto, Cosmo Leonardo, Pat Orecchio, Reuben Cohen, Guido Casa and Richie DiPaolo.

Columbus pizza culture has led innovation in the pizza business and, at its peak, rightfully earned Columbus the title of Pizza Capital of the United States from *Pizza Today Magazine* for several years. Columbus has been a place of innovation for the industry as a whole. Spinoff businesses from Jim Grote, the founder of Donatos, have grown technology that has transformed pizza shops and the frozen pizza industry. Now a local supplier to pizza shops and all types of food businesses, the former DiPaolo Foods, now RDP, has shaped the industry by advocating for new products and supporting the local pizza industry in countless ways since the dawn of pizzerias in the 1950s. The Ezzo Sausage Company, working with local shop owners to find new and more efficient versions of pepperoni, has risen from a small family business to a cutting-edge industry leader known across the world. While residents of Columbus might not know how important the city is to pizza, the industry continues to look to Columbus for trends and innovations.

This passion for pizza continues to this day, fueled by the spirit and determination of small mom-and-pop pizza shops. The heritage was shaped by a handful of first- and second-generation immigrant entrepreneurs often working during the day and slinging pizza pies at night. The connection to the past has been sustained by second-, third- and fourth-generation family members, surviving and thriving supported by a customer base of legions of loyal guests who have often become second family members over the decades. These shops, in turn, sponsored countless little league teams, school fundraisers, community events and area churches. A defining characteristic of the pizza business in this town is the longevity of employees and salespeople. Unique to the food service world, many of these family businesses have staff that have worked behind the counter for decades. These businesses have worked with salespeople from places like RDP for entire careers. There is a pizza community in Columbus that is unique—more than a guild or trade organization—it is a special culture that was created in the early days and sustains today. How did this happen in the most middle-of-the-road midwestern town?

Ultimately, this is a story of assimilating immigrants creating a lasting legacy. There are countless special stories and elements to this culture of pizza in Columbus, and we will explore all of them in the pages to come. If you came to this book looking for a best-of list or a detailed Yelp-style review of your personal top ten favorite pizza places of all time, I

Empty pizza boxes stacked high at Pizza Grand Prix IV, which was voted the best event of 2009 on Columbus Underground. *Courtesy Bethia Woolf, Columbus Food Adventures.*

apologize, you might be disappointed. There are hundreds of pizzerias in Columbus today. Over the course of seventy-plus years, there have been over one thousand pizza businesses. Some have survived to the current generation, many have changed hands over the years and a good number were casualties of time—the loss of a patriarch or matriarch or changing demographics of their communities.

You will not find all of the best pizza places here—there are still too many to count—but you will read about the stories of some of the best people in the pizza business. I also hope that this book will whet your appetite to seeking out a new mom-and-pop shop that needs your support and that it will renew your loyalty for your neighborhood favorite. There is a chance that pizza as we know it in Columbus might not survive to the next generation. My hope is that if enough people read this book, we can collectively support and sustain these quintessential small businesses and preserve Columbus-style pizza.

1

PRIMORDIAL PIZZA

Pizza as we know it has evolved over thousands of years. Dough with olive oil and a sprinkling of herbs has existed throughout the Mediterranean since Roman times. The next pizza progression was the arrival of the Indian Water Buffalo to Sicily and Italy in the Middle Ages, which led to mozzarella di buffalo becoming an essential pizza topping. The citizens of Naples started to integrate tomatoes into their daily cuisine in the eighteenth century, which was followed by the first pizzerias in the 1830s. Naples remains the epicenter of Italian pizza to this day. Pizza Margherita (mozzarella di buffalo, basil and tomatoes), which by legend, is based on the colors of the Italian flag, was all the rage in certain parts of Italy in the 1890s, when Italian immigrants started to make their way to Columbus. Many came from a few villages in the Abruzzo region of Italy to work in the stone quarries in the Marble Cliff area. These immigrants brought their version of pizza with them.

Early memories of pizza in Columbus are very similar. Jimmy Corrova of TAT Ristorante remembers pizza as a family snack. His mother was from Naples, and she brought her pizza traditions with her. Children were given leftover dough to play with. They would roll it and flatten it, then squeeze tomatoes on top, add some basil and cook the combination on an open hearth. Rita (Mizer), Dick and Paul DiPaolo (DiPaolo Foods and RDP) recall Grandmother DiPaolo making what was called pizza bread, which included olive oil, fresh tomatoes squeezed by hand and maybe some grated romano cheese if it was available. Throughout Columbus, pizza, which was sometimes called tomato pie, would have been found in the immigrant homes of Flytown, St. Clair Avenue, San Margherita and Grandview during the 1920s and 1930s. During the Great Depression, cheese was often a luxury, so it took a long time for pizza to transform from a family snack to a featured menu item.

In the world of food history, the first place to serve a particular item in any city is often hotly contested. In the case of Columbus, all sources agree. The first pizza served outside of a home was at TAT Ristorante as early as 1934. Jimmy Corrova is the second-generation owner of TAT today, and his childhood memory of the pizza served at TAT in the 1940s remains vivid. The dough was one inch thick. It was placed in a fourteen-inch Bluebird Pie Pan (from the Bluebird Pie Pan Company on the west side of Columbus). Cornmeal was dusted on the bottom of the pan to keep the dough from sticking. House-made tomato sauce with oregano and garlic was ladled on top. Then six to eight one-inch square slices of American cheese were placed over the sauce. Pepperoni was not widely available or used as a pizza topping during this era, so the topping of choice was often anchovies. Jimmy still fondly recalls the anchovies of this time because they were fresh—not out of a can—and added a real flavor to pizza served at TAT. The pizza was then cut into squares, which was called tavern cut. When it was made for carryout, the pizza was placed on a cardboard square and slid into a paper bag. However, pizza was still not commonly known outside of the Italian community of Columbus and was not a featured menu item. Columbus phone books of the late 1940s to 1954 listed pizza as a category in the bakery section of the city listings. Searching through those old ads, you can find only a few bakeries that listed pizza as an item, and it appears to have been offered as dough, not as a finished product to serve.

Pizza is still served at TAT today. The story of TAT Ristorante begins in 1929 in the former Flytown neighborhood of Columbus at 409 West Goodale Street. Pete and Philomena Corrova were looking for a name for their new restaurant. Prior to opening the doors to the public, a historic event occurred at the city's airport, the Columbus Municipal Hangar (CMH) on the east side. On July 9, 1929, the first transcontinental flights in the United States were launched. Passengers started their journey in New York via train. The first stop was Columbus, where train passengers were transferred to a waiting Ford Tri-Motor aircraft to fly them to their next destination. In the course of forty-eight hours, a person could travel from New York to Los Angeles. It was an amazing feat for the time and the talk of the town that Columbus was part of it. The name of this new

Exterior of the original TAT Ristorante, circa 1950. Jimmy Corrova (*left*) and Richard Corrova (*right*). *Courtesy of Corrova family.*

airline was Transcontinental Air Transport or T-A-T. Legend says that Pete Corrova would watch planes from Transcontinental Air Transport flying into and out from the airport and decided to use the initials he saw on the planes as the name of the restaurant.

Another legend suggests that officials from T-A-T once came by to ask about the use of the name, and Pete replied that it stood for "take any table." The airline did not last long and faded from memory quickly, and we do know that Pete's son Jimmy Corrova started to tell customers that TAT indeed stood for take any table. Today, the current home for TAT features a wonderful mural by local artist Carl Weisenberger depicting the history of TAT, the airline, in a series of images.

"Progress" in the form of new highways cut up the Flytown neighborhood in the early 1950s and forced TAT to move. Pete and Philomena opened the new location on the growing east side at 3280 East Main Street at South Hampton Road, and it remained there until 1965. The couple continued to serve food that reflected Pete's Sicilian (Ficara) roots and the recipes

Mural depicting the story of Transcontinental Air Transport at TAT Ristorante. *Courtesy of Jodi Miller Photography.*

Philomena brought from Naples and, of course, pizza. In 1955 or 1954, Jimmy Corrova and his wife, Dolores, opened a second TAT at East Broad Street and James Road. In 1962, the family added a location at Livingston Avenue and Beechwood Road. This was followed by a pizza-focused location on the west side, the TAT Pizza Carry Out at 3858 Sullivant Avenue (which became Minelli's Restaurant & Pizza Carry Out in 1967). During its brief tenure as a TAT, the west side location was very busy. Jimmy Corrova recalled that they used "five to six delivery wagons and sold six hundred pizzas per night on Friday and Saturday." After the death of patriarch Pete, followed by Jimmy having a heart attack, the family decided to merge the two remaining east side TATs in 1980, which remains TAT's location today at 1210 South James Road at Livingston Avenue.

As the oldest continuously owned family restaurant in Columbus, with over ninety years of service, a plethora of memories and stories have accumulated. In accordance with a tradition followed by most of the original pizzerias and many Italian restaurants in town, recipes are not written down. Kitchen staff (or family members) are shown how to make something and then they follow suit. Before Jimmy had heart surgery in the 1980s, he made sure that video tapes were made showing him creating all of the essential recipes for the kitchen.

Corrova started working at TAT when he was seven. When he was nine, he stood on a crate to run the cash register. Today, his wife, Dolores, is the general manager and his brother Anthony is the maître d'. Defying generations of Sicilian tradition of leaving everything to the firstborn son, his daughters Michelle (back of house/kitchen) and Marianne (front of house) are ready to take over the family business when Jimmy decides to give up the reins.

A favorite story of Jimmy Corrova involves his David versus Goliath fight with several big businesses in his cease and desist lawsuit involving the use of the term "Poor Boy" sandwiches in Ohio. At the time, several companies, including Kroger, were selling frozen Poor Boy sandwiches locally. A barely adult Jimmy decided to bring a lawsuit against these companies, including the local grocery store chain. Shortly after, word got out about what he was planning to do, and he was asked to meet with "a few people" at Romeo's Pizzeria. When he arrived, the place was full of various Italian community leaders, as well as powerful Democratic and Republican lawmakers. He was very strongly "encouraged" to stop his legal fight to avoid stirring up the pot. He was told that the suit would destroy the family business and be bad for the Italian American community. Afterward, he went to church, where he "received a message from heaven" that he would win the case. When he asked his lawyer how much he should sue for, he was told $100,000. He recalls thinking that was a lot of zeros. He did win the case after six years, and TAT still owns the Poor Boy trademark to this day. Jimmy believes the headline in the *Citizen Journal* (local newspaper of the time) on the day he won the lawsuit was "Judge Slices Up Sandwich Attorneys."

TAT is known for having many employees who have worked front and back of house for decades, as well as countless regular customers who span the generations. Many customers have a favorite booth and/or server. One booth even has a plaque dedicated to a longtime customer who passed away; now her seat is reserved for her forever. TAT puts the old into old school in every aspect one can imagine. This family business has survived the Great Depression, countless recessions, trends, fads and an endless stream of new competition by not changing a thing. The only thing that has changed at TAT is its style of pizza, which has evolved from the original thicker crust interpretation with American cheese to the classic Columbus-style, with just a few tweaks since the 1950s.

2

PIONEERS OF COLUMBUS PIZZA (1950–54)

The first pizzeria in the United States was Lombardi's, which opened in New York City in 1904. Pizzerias started to pop up along the Northeast coast in the 1920s and early 1930s. Other areas with large Italian American communities in the Midwest, such as Chicago, saw pizzerias start to open in the mid-1930s. By the end of the 1940s, pizza was known in some communities but was still well off the culinary radar of the typical American. Food legend and lore suggests that American soldiers developed a taste for pizza during World War II while in Italy. That might be true, but considering the citizens of war-torn Italy had meager resources, it is unlikely that there was a plethora of pizza to be experienced by most soldiers. More likely, it was servicemen stationed there after the war in the 1950s who started to seek out pizza on their return home. This author believes that a driving force of pizza interest was sparked by soldiers and sailors returning from World War II via New York City, who likely experienced an Americanized version of pizza and saw how well it was selling to the masses. The entrepreneurial spirit and the prosperity of the 1950s fueled the growth of pizza across the country as the decade progressed. The advent of the gas-fired Bakers Pride pizza oven in 1945 and reliable and affordable Hobart mixers made making more pizza easier and more profitable. As for the Buckeye State, Columbus might have been the first city to serve pizza in Ohio. It was definitely among the first cities in the Midwest to embrace pizza and was one of the fastest-growing pizza markets from the 1950s to the beginning of the twenty-first century.

ROMEO'S (1950)

The first pizzeria in Columbus was Romeo's. It opened in December 1950 at the corner of West Fifth Avenue and North Star Road. The tagline of its later advertising stated, "Since…1950 The Year Columbus Discovered Pizza." The restaurant was quickly the talk of the town. Soon Romeo's was serving up to two hundred pizzas per day. Pizza was such a foreign concept that local columnist Richard Rodgers had to spell it phonetically, "pete-sah," with emphasis on the "pete," in a 1951 article about the growing trend in the capital city. Romeo's had a prime location for growth; it was near the heart of the local Italian community, and both owners lived nearby. Sandwiched between Upper Arlington High School and Grandview Heights High School, Romeo's quickly became the destination for teenage socializing. Teens loved this new, easy-to-share menu offering served at the table on red-and-white checkerboard tablecloths. Adults loved the option to pick up (in a paper bag) an affordable dinner for the family on the way home from work. Teens and adults alike valued the late-night hours of Romeo's (3:30 a.m. on Friday and Saturday), which offered a rare afterhours dining and socializing option that few places in the city offered for all ages.

The initial version of pizza was very different from what it became over time. The first pizzas at Romeo's had a crust that was thicker than the typical Columbus style of today. Grated romano cheese was sprinkled lightly over the slightly sweet tomato sauce with a strong dash of oregano. Customers had to ask for sliced mozzarella cheese as an additional topping. Hand-sliced pepperoni was a featured topping. Most people credit Romeo's as the first place in Columbus to serve this unique American spin on Italian sausage, as it was not a widely used food in Columbus until the pizzeria opened. The profuse use of pepperoni as a topping quickly became a signature of Romeo's (and Columbus pizza in general). Over time, mozzarella and provolone became more prominent as the default base for pizzas in in the city. Massey shifted to provolone as his preferred cheese for his tomato pies in a few years.

The duo behind Romeo's paired Jimmie Massey (he changed his name from Massucci) with Romeo Sirij. The two met in Columbus sometime in the 1940s. Sirij was originally from New Jersey. His father was a pizza maker in Naples who later opened a pizzeria in New York. In the late 1930s, Sirij came to Columbus on a two-week vacation, met the girl of his dreams and decided to stay. They married in 1941. Sirij worked a variety of jobs in Columbus and had a series of business ventures, but he was best known as a wine salesman for the Militello Macaroni Company. Jimmy Carrova of TAT

Romeo's Pizza menu from early 1950s.

believes that Sirij, while dropping in on sales calls at his restaurant, might have been inspired to start a pizzeria after seeing how well pizza was selling at TAT.

Jimmie Massey was born in Chicago in 1901. He worked as a baker in Chicago and Detroit. Massey had relatives with a pizza place in Chicago, and he may have worked there occasionally. He came from a long line of bakers: his grandfather Giuseppe Antonio DiMichele owned the Detroit Italian Baking Company. Massey's path to Columbus was not unlike his pizza muse Romeo; he met his future wife while visiting friends. Massey became a permanent resident in 1939 after marrying Martha Cosentino at St. Patrick Church on Thanksgiving Day. In the early 1940s, he worked at the Garden Restaurant near Grant Hospital, and in the restaurant kitchen, he would sometimes make his version pizza as an off-menu item for some of the dining doctors. Sirij and Massey were uniquely qualified to open the first pizzeria in Columbus when they paired up to open Romeo's.

Considering the red sauced fare that Massey was creating, it is interesting that he did not like tomatoes, and when making a pizza for himself, it was always his special version of white pizza. However, he was very proud and particular about his tomato sauce. He made one version for pizza and another, with a slight spicy kick, for pasta sauce. Massey would even insist on using his own sauce when dinner was served for visitors at his home, even if he had to drop off some from the restaurant and then head back to work.

Later in the 1950s, Romeo's would add a second location on the Ohio State University campus at the rear of 278 West Lane Avenue (the back section of present-day Varsity Club). This carryout pizzeria across from St. John Arena, which brought in tournament fans from across Ohio, exposed many to their first pizza. Jimmy Massey would leave Romeo's after several years to work on other pizza projects. Romeo's continued to be an area favorite through the 1970s in spite of having to move farther west on Fifth Avenue when the restaurant lost its prime location to a gas station. To this day, many people in Columbus have fond memories about Romeo's as the first place they shared pizza with friends.

Massey's Pizza (1951)

Jimmy Massey quickly established himself as a pizza pro in central Ohio. He worked with his brother Dan (one of his eight siblings) to start Massey's Pizza at 4464 East Main Street in Whitehall in 1951. The location placed the pizzeria in a prime location, and it was an immediate hit. Later in the 1950s, he set up his own eponymous location, Jimmy Massey's Drive-In, at 1941 Livingston Avenue. Massey's son, Father Joseph D. Massucci, recalls that there was a butcher shop a short distance from the drive-in. His father would take a big bag of spices over with him to have a special base sausage blend made for him. He had two versions of sausage produced—one for pizza and a spicy version for sandwiches. This location had a good run for several years but ended up closing in the early 1960s.

Massey helped a relative start a pizzeria in Cleveland. He also set up a Lancaster location in 1961 with Red "Bud" Combine, a local personality and his wife's cousin. Massey always loved the hospitality aspect of the business and talking with customers. When he "retired" from his own pizzerias, he still had the business in his blood. In 1981, at the age of eighty, he could be found making pizzas part-time at the Varsity Club in a space that was formerly the second Romeo's location.

Massey's pizza has remained a Columbus institution to this day. We will discuss more of the evolution of Massey's in later chapters.

Massey's Pizza Yellow Pages ads, circa 1959.

Tommy's Pizza (1952)

Thomas (Tommy) Iacono's family were immigrants from Sicily. He grew up in Silver Creek, New York, helping his father cater parties and weddings. He found himself in Columbus after a stint in the army in World War II. When he opened his first pizzeria in 1952, he brought the family recipes that he and his father had developed over the years. The original location of Tommy's was at 2729 East Fifth Avenue at Cassidy Avenue. The legendary *Dispatch* food writer Doral Chenoweth (known as the Grumpy Gourmet) noted in a 1989 article that he had his first pizza at this location, and it served pizza only. He frequently wrote about Tommy's over the years. Chenoweth also noted that the first version of Tommy's pizza was thicker than what is served today. In the early days of the pizzeria, Iacono rolled pie crusts using a wringer for a washing machine from his former dry-cleaning business.

In 1963, Iacono opened a second location in Upper Arlington at Lane Avenue and North Star Avenue. The first version was essentially a cottage to serve pizza. It was very small with a handful of tables. In 1967, a new building was constructed at 1350 West Lane Avenue, with more additions over time. This location became the flagship location for Tommy's in subsequent decades. The West Lane location also served as Iacono's office as he grew the business. Originally called Tommy's Restaurant, the name was changed to Tommy's Pizza once the pizza boom showed that it was not going to go bust.

The reach of Tommy's Pizza expanded slowly over the years. A third location opened shortly after, at 1430 South Hamilton Road, which was a neighborhood favorite on the east side for decades, before it closed in 2014. In 1978, a Tommy's opened at the corner of Neil and Lane Avenues (174 West Lane Avenue), expanding and securing even stronger ties to the Ohio State University campus. In the mid-1980s, a fifth location opened in Dublin at 4279 West Dublin Granville Road. Over time, Iacono shared ownership of the Hamilton Road location, and another at 3020 East Broad Street, with manager and partner Jim Gillilan. Eventually, Gillilan bought the rights to the Broad Street location and shared it with his son. Iacono's son Rick now runs the two Lane Avenue spots and the Dublin location.

Tommy Iacono passed away on December 31, 1998. All of the restaurants were closed for the funeral, with pallbearers including longtime employees like Joe Roesch. His obituary recorded "vegetable gardening, golf and work" as Iacono's passions. Iacono was known for his huge garden, and he often shared fresh tomatoes with his employees and used them in his sauces.

While there have been several Tommy's locations over the years, when people reminisce about Tommy's, they often think about one of the two on Lane Avenue. Many customers were introduced to Tommy's while attending classes at OSU or home football games. Many residents of Upper Arlington have made West Lane Tommy's Pizza a family tradition over the decades.

The same holds true for Dublin Tommy's fans. Ask most customers, and they will insist theirs is the best.

While nationally the top five days for pizza sales are Super Bowl Sunday, New Year's Eve, Halloween, the night before Thanksgiving and New Year's Day, the Lane Avenue locations cause an aberration because Ohio State University home football games are the biggest sales days of the year. The West Lane location will see profit add up to double the normal Saturday sales. The campus location will do up to four to six times the business of a normal Saturday. While National Championship games are large draws, the big sales day is any home game, especially an OSU versus Michigan game, when played at the stadium. It has been a tradition at the campus location to sell subs in the parking lot to people attending the game. This was a tradition that Tommy Iacono often participated in. During the 2002 championship game, Tommy's same day shipped subs to Tempe, Arizona. Per Manager Brock Saulters, "A former employee's family who had gone to watch the game *had* to have Tommy's subs on game day."

Exterior of Tommy's Pizza, opened in 1978, at Lane and Neil Avenue across from Ohio State campus.

There are countless traditions that have developed at Tommy's over the years. Cardboard pizza rounds are taped to the walls of the West Lane location, showcasing signatures from famous customers, including OSU coaches and players. The two Lane Avenue locations have employees who have worked there for three or four decades, and many multigenerational families have been Tommy's loyalists since the 1960s. The longest held tradition, which dates back to the first location, is house-made sausage, which continues to be a favorite pizza topping to this day, as well as house-made meatballs for pastas and pizzas. Both use the original recipe from the 1950s.

GATTO'S PIZZA (1952)

Gatto's Pizza was founded in 1952 by brothers Jimmy and Joe Gatto. It is the oldest continuously operated pizzeria in Columbus. Gatto's has been owned by the same family at the same location since its founding. Without an ounce of exaggeration, you cannot create a place like this anymore. There are a few pizza shops that have a slightly longer history, but the Gatto's are among our founding families of pizza.

Mounted on the wall is a large black-and-white photo showing the view out Gatto's front window taken shortly after the business opened. Today, while looking hard at the photo, one will see little has changed from that opening day in 1952. The original Vulcan gas oven was replaced by two newer models to increase production, and the business started taking credit cards in June 2019; otherwise, you could still be in the 1950s. The majority of the employees over the years have been Gatto children, cousins and close friends, which has continued a persistent family atmosphere in the pizzeria.

The founding Gattos grew up in Flytown, the Italian part of Columbus, which is largely the Short North today. Joe's family was living on the south side (near the original Donatos of the 1960s), when they opened the pizza shop. "It was Uncle Jimmy's idea, and they chose Clintonville because the north side was growing," says Vince Gatto, a second-generation Gatto who runs the shop today. Jimmy had experience working in bars, and the family as a whole had a lot of restaurant experience.

Vince started working at Gatto's when he was ten, wiping pans and rolling dough. He took the bus from the south side to Clintonville every Friday and Saturday to work until he was old enough to drive. Vince, his brother

Joe (Joe Gatto II) and a cousin, Bill Fulcher (whose mother was a Gatto), bought the business from Joe and Jimmy in 1983, after years of working in the shop. At the time, all three had full time jobs, so they divided up days and responsibilities to keep the pizzeria going. Vince took over many of the operational duties of Gatto's in 1993, when he was one of fifty thousand employees laid off from Sears on the same day. In 2019, Joe II was no longer at Gatto's, and Don came in about once per week.

Vince says there are too many stories to tell from being a family-run business in the same neighborhood for almost seventy years; however, one day does stand out. In the early 2000s, a hurricane-force storm struck Columbus, and especially Clintonville, hard, causing the area to lose power for hours. Vince had the day off, and he had started it with a memorable day of golf with friends. He decided to check on Gatto's because of the storm. When he called in, he was told that they were getting ready to close the store because the power was out. Vince told the employee to "stay open and keep answering the phone" and he would be right there. He spent the rest of the day rolling dough by hand (like the old days) and

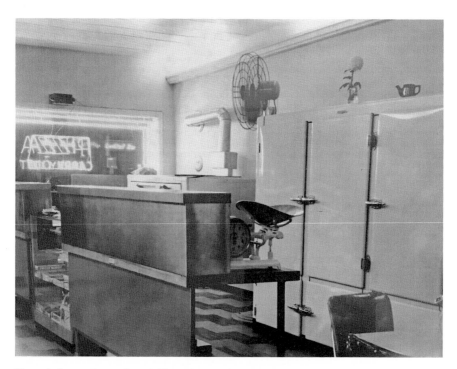

Framed photo taken at Gatto's Pizza shortly after opening in 1952.

Participants at a sausage making party at Gatto's Pizza.

prepping pizza, which they could still cook in their gas ovens. It ended up being one of the busiest days ever, since no one else was open. By the end of the day, they had little product left, which was great, since they had no working refrigeration.

A great Gatto's tradition is the annual Sausage Party, which started in the late 1990s. Every year during the third week of December, a collection of friends, family and longtime customers gather to spend a day making Gatto's sausage, often around three to four hundred pounds. Everyone takes some home to serve for the holidays.

The sausage recipe hails from Sicily and was handed down to the pizza shop by Vince's grandfather. As is often the case in Italian and Sicilian sausage recipes, the mix has a hearty dose of fennel, the common denominator for the handful of longtime Columbus pizza purveyors who still make their own sausage. When asked why he continues this labor-intensive endeavor, Vince responded that he has tasted commercial sausages over the years but has never found anything he thought tasted better. Another unique property of the sausage used on the pizza is cutting it into rectangular slices instead of placing it on the cheese as crumbles.

Gatto's makes its own dough, meatballs, sauce and the only salad dressing offered, Italian, from scratch. It is a hands-on, labor-intensive business, following a model no new pizzeria would use. Today, the challenges of continuing the legacy are changing eating preferences, more competition, less available parking and the nearby demographic of grad students and new residents who do not have the same tradition of going to Gatto's by default. Those who have not discovered Gatto's are missing out on good food and a true time-capsule experience. Those who grew up with Gatto's would benefit by ordering a pizza to rediscover the shop and to confirm that nothing has changed over the decades.

LEONARDO'S PIZZA (1953)

The last of the original Leonardo's Pizza locations closed in the 1990s. Many people still fondly recall Leonardo's and seek out pizza like what they remember being served. Leonardo's was started by Patrick and Anna Rose Orecchio with Cosmo and Rosemary Leonardo. The first version of the pizzeria briefly operated inside the Orecchio's house on Northwest Boulevard in Grandview. It soon moved just down the street to 1045 West First Avenue, near the corner of Copeland Road, in a small building that offered drive-in and delivery service.

Cosmo Leonardo left the business to pursue his dream of being a professional drummer and leader of the Love Notes, a band that entertained people throughout Ohio for years. The Orecchios continued to grow and expand the business in a very short period of time, with locations throughout Columbus.

Leonardo's quickly became the first and largest pizzeria chain in Columbus—an accomplishment it would hold for many decades. By 1969, there were seven Leonardo's locations in Columbus. At the peak of the brand, there were nine locations—a number that Donatos did not see until the early 1980s. The most important legacy of Leonardo's is the training ground it became for future pizza shop owners, including Nick Panzera, Phillip Panzera and Paul Lombardi (Panzera's); Joe Apollino (Dante's); Jed and Dave Pallone (Massey's); Bob Snyder (Antolino's); and countless others.

The Leonardo's name appeared in other forms in later years. Cosmo and Rosemary's son Steve used family recipes to open two pizzerias: Leo's

Rubino's sign in daylight.

Downtown Pizza and Steve Leonardo's Pizza. Patrick and Anna Rose Orecchio's son Drew opened the Original Leonardo's Pizza in 2013 on Hague Avenue. It was only open for about one year but had rave reviews from those who recalled the original.

Rubino's (1954)

In 1954, Ruben Cohen opened Rubino's Pizza in a two-story brick building in Bexley at 2643 East Main Street, at the corner of South Roosevelt Avenue. Little, if anything, has changed since 1954. Rubino's is still a cash-only business. If you want to time travel to 1954 to see how pizza was made then, walk through the doors of Rubino's to view mid-century pizza technology and technique, down to serving carryout pizza in white paper bags formed into a tent. The menu remains simple and unchanged, although one unlikely option—perhaps a remnant of a bygone fad or preview of the future—is pickles as a topping. Legend has it that the Bexley High School marching band played in the parking lot on opening day. Regulars have called the place Rube's since the beginning.

Bexley native Bob Greene has written in depth about Rubino's in countless newspaper articles about his youth growing up in Bexley. In his book *Be True to Your School,* Greene documented a year in his high school life that included at least ten trips to Rubino's. Longtime Bob Greene fans have made pilgrimages to Rubino's to re-create the nostalgia of the 1950s and 1960s. Another famous customer is also a writer, R.L. Stine. He lives in New York but is such a fan of the pizza of his youth that he flies in several times per year.

Regulars call the place Rube's, but friends often called Rubino Ruby. Reuben lived above the shop for many years. Before the pizzeria, he was a salesperson for a belt company and a boxer in the navy. It is said that he discovered pizza while in New York City. Paul DiPaolo (DiPaolo Foods/ RDP) recalls his first phone call to Ruby to take an order. He gave four

Rubino's Pizza with extra cheese, pepperoni and sausage cooked well done.

items and then Ruby hung up the phone. Paul went to his dad and said, "Ruby hung up on me, what am I supposed to do?" Richie DiPaolo said, "That is just Ruby deciding to take care of a customer coming through the door, he will call back later to add to the order." The same dedication to the customer continues to this day.

Two early employees were Frank Marchese and Tom Cully. The two were part of the group that purchased Rubino's in 1988, when Cohen retired to Florida. Frank Marchese was very much a part of Rubino's, running the operation for Cohen for decades. He started, at least on a part-time basis, as early as 1955. Marchese also worked at two other notable Columbus spots in the 1950s—the original Jai Lai and the Desert Inn. Frank led the charge in 1983 to save Rubino's from being sold to develop a meat market. By getting plenty of local support from longtime fans, the community was able to stop the sale and continue the tradition of Rubino's for another generation.

Cohen passed away in 1998, and Frank Marchese died a few years later. In the twenty-first century, Rubino's has been operated by Jim, Mark and Karen Marchese, who continue to not change a thing. The business is largely from Bexley-based regulars who frequently do not have to state their order because the staff behind the counter already know what it is. Regulars know to order a classic Rubino's pie in this manner: order the pie "single cut" (like it used to be served in the '50s, '60s and part of the '70s) and well done, with extra cheese, pepperoni and sausage. If you are dining in, you can expect your order to be paired with a Styrofoam cup and a can of pop. The cup might have been paper in the 1950s and the pop might have been a quarter, but otherwise, Rubino's is unchanged. And speaking of change, it is still cash only. Luckily, there are ATMs nearby.

THE EVOLUTION OF COLUMBUS-STYLE PIZZA

The original versions of pizza served in Columbus in the early 1950s were very different from what was found all over town just a few years later. In a short time, a variety of pizza started to emerge, which became a defined style by the mid-1950s. A combination of factors created this Columbus version of pizza. Many of the new pizzerias were started by former employees or relatives of the original pizzerias. Richie DiPaolo was a local grocer who started to deliver pizza ingredients to shops all over town. Having a supplier dedicated to pizza led to some standardization of ingredients, as well as some innovations.

Finally, by the mid-1950s, Columbus pizza was kneaded and shaped into the style it is today: thin to almost medium flakey crust; cut in squares or long rectangles (tavern cut or party cut); tomato sauce with a slight sweetness; a preference for grated provolone or a provolone mozzarella cheese blend; a strong focus on toppings, especially our local need for a plethora of pepperoni; and a dusting of cornmeal on the bottom (cornmeal is less common as pizza ovens and cooking techniques have evolved).

There have been other changes in how we serve pizza. Until the 1970s, if you wanted to order green peppers on a pizza, you would ask for mangoes. Pizza was served in paper bags originally. (You can still find this at Rubino's.) Many pizza places made their own blend of sausage based on old world family recipes. At least eight still follow that tradition: Iacono's, Gatto's, Terita's, Rubino's, Borgata, TAT, Tommy's and Enrico's.

3

PILLARS OF PIZZA

Many individuals grew and shaped the pizza culture of Columbus. First and foremost is Richard "Richie" DiPaolo Sr. Next is the informal guild and information exchange for pizza parlor owners, the American Italian Golf Association. Finally, the culture and support of the early Italian American neighborhoods provided the networks, camaraderie and locations for the first pizzerias in Columbus. The 1950s was the time for Italian Americans to be accepted in mainstream culture. Dean Martin's "That's Amore"—with the now famous line "when the moon hits your eye like a big pizza pie, that's amore!"—was a top hit in 1953 and helped promote pizza to the masses.

AMERICAN ITALIAN GOLF ASSOCIATION

It may come as a surprise, but golf played an important part in the business of pizza in Columbus. Joe Gatto (founder of Gatto's) and Romeo Sirij (who started the first pizzeria in Columbus) were best friends since their Flytown days and continued to be frequent visitors to each other's businesses and homes throughout their lives. Tommy Iacono (Tommy's Pizza) and Joe Gatto were also great friends, who saw each other almost daily when they retired and played golf together for decades. A binding part of the original Columbus pizza community was that most of the shop owners from the

1950s and 1960s, as well as their suppliers, grew up together in the same tight-knit neighborhoods, attended the same churches and frequented the clubhouse and the links of the American Italian Golf Association when they could slice out a day off. They might not have worked together, but they did enjoy playing together and talking shop on the course.

In the 1930s and 1940s, many Italian teenagers were caddies at local golf clubs. While they were welcome as caddies, the unwritten rules of the day did not encourage them or their fathers to play golf at the courses. On Sundays, the young caddies would often meet with their families to dine on spaghetti and meatballs under the shade of trees during breaks in play. After serving in World War II, many of these former caddies wanted to return to golf. A reunion of former caddies led to the formation of the American Italian Golf Club in 1947, with the first golf tournament held at Indian Springs Golf Course on October 12, 1947. The driving force behind the club was "master caddy" Pat Guidi, who had served as a mentor to the other caddies for years and arranged informal tournaments for them.

Members of the DiPaolo family and customers at their St. Clair Avenue shop. Rita DiPaolo and Richie DiPaolo are on the far right. *Courtesy of DiPaolo family.*

Membership was limited to men of Italian heritage and their sons. The founding members, numbering 240, paid three dollars to join the group. More members joined in the 1950s and 1960s as a new wave of immigrants arrived from the Abruzzi region of Italy. Eugene Riccardi (Riccardi's Restaurant) was the 1960 District Amateur Golf Champion in Columbus. His win earned a photo in the *Dispatch*, which showed him being congratulated by his business partner, Guido Casa.

The American Italian Golf Association had short-term locations in the 1950s and 1960s, before buying a farm on the northwest side of town, near Dublin. The Riviera Country Club and golf course officially opened on June 15, 1970. There were many stone markers set by trees (recalling the spaghetti dinners of years past) with the names of families from the association who helped build parts of the course. Interesting traditions developed over time. When the Gatto's played golf, it was tradition to have a shot of Crown Royale at the fourteenth hole. Tommy Iacono lived nearby, enjoying the short commute to his favorite golf course. The regulars at the course included many local pizzeria owners, and membership grew to four hundred. The course and clubhouse were sold in 2015 to make room for "progress." The American Italian Golf Association continues to this day and still includes a who's who of local dough slingers.

Richie DiPaolo/DiPaolo Foods/RDP

In 1915, Luisa DiPaolo used a railroad bonus that her husband, Paolo, received to open a small grocery store in a basement on St. Clair Avenue to serve the largely Italian American community of immigrants clustered in that part of town. Paolo joined in the business a few years later when there was a strike at the railroad where he worked. When the strike was over, he worked days at the store and nights for the railroad. When Luisa died in 1922, her children worked with their father to keep the store going. One of the children, Richie, started stocking shelves when he was eight years old. As Richie grew older, he took on a larger role so that his father could continue the family business and move the DiPaolo Food Shoppe to a new, larger location that was still on St. Clair Avenue.

The store faced hard times throughout the Great Depression and World War II, but the business held on and even earned the loyalty of customers by extending lines of credit for those facing hard times. However, the

Exterior of DiPaolo Food Shoppe in the 1930s. *Courtesy of DiPaolo family.*

neighborhood was changing due to postwar prosperity, which allowed many residents to move to the growing suburbs. There was also disruption from a new highway cutting up central neighborhoods, including St. Clair Avenue. As a way to attract more business, Richie started delivering to restaurants as a value-added service for some customers in the late 1940s. Inspired by the rapid growth of pizzerias opened by many of his friends and customers, in 1957, Richie shifted from the grocery business and officially opened DiPaolo Food Distributors with the goal to expand his food distribution business throughout the city.

The company started with a focus on supplying the needs of the continually growing pizza businesses in Columbus. Owners benefited from having supplies delivered to their kitchens instead of having to shop and pick up supplies. Since many of these new businesses were only open in the evening and the owners often had day jobs, the option to have delivery was priceless. Richie did more than sell cheese and toppings, he also helped shape the local industry with advice, innovation and, more often than can be counted, letting new or struggling businesses take order on credit or even offering a small loan. Richie was more than a salesman to these entrepreneurs;

he was a friend and confidante. His children tell stories of many a Friday night when he would load up the family car after dinner with his wife and children and deliver to local pizza shops preparing for the weekend. It was not uncommon for his family to wait in the car for over an hour while Richie chatted or problem solved with pizzeria owners inside. The family waited in the car, often in the not-so-nice parts of town. Dipaolo was still a shrewd businessman. Pizzerias were cash-only businesses at the time, so it was a sure thing that his customers would have money for payment on a Friday night.

DiPaolo Foods introduced several innovations to the Columbus pizza community. In the early days, carryout pizza was placed in a paper bag. As orders grew larger on busy Friday and Saturday nights, pizzerias looked for easier ways for delivery drivers and customers to transport and stack pizzas. Some pizzerias tried using donut and bakery boxes. Richie worked with the Columbus Carton Company to start making pizza boxes for the community. The original boxes were yellow instead of white.

The business offered extra services to customers who lacked the equipment, space or time for certain jobs. The DiPaolos sliced pepperoni for customers who did not have slicers, grated romano cheese in massive quantities and shredded provolone, which was becoming the dominant cheese for Columbus pizza in the 1950s.

Customers started asking for pre-sliced peppers so that they would not have to deal with seeds, juice from the peppers and the pain of getting that juice in a cut or nicked finger. After much trial and error, Richie finally asked the Vlasic Pickle Company if it could provide sliced peppers using specialized equipment. Vlasic could not use its regular slicers on peppers but figured out how to do it with a pickle slicer. The result was the distinct look and flavor of sliced banana peppers/hot pepper rings. This was one of the top selling items for Vlasic for years. Initial response to this new type of topping was lukewarm, but after a campus sub shop started asking for multiple jars, banana peppers took off as additions to pizza and subs.

When pepperoni became all the rage in Columbus (including the Columbus style of blanketing a pizza with pepperoni from center to crust), Richie found a meat packer to increase pepperoni slices to the width of a silver dollar to make it easier to "dress the pie."

DiPaolo also brought Sausage for Pizza (SFP) to Columbus through one of the packing companies he worked with. SFP was specially created for the pizza market.

Dick and Paul DiPaolo recall working hard for their dad while growing up. Two memories stand out: having twenty-four hours to unload three

Richie DiPaolo and his wife, Josephine. *Courtesy of DiPaolo family.*

thousand cases of tomatoes from rail cars and their dad "helping" them. He lubricated a conveyor belt with olive oil, which made it so fast that Paul and Dick could not keep up with the onslaught of items coming at them.

The company continued to grow until 1985, when it received an offer it could not refuse. The largest foodservice company in North America, SYSCO, offered to buy the family business, including the opportunity for family members to stay as part of the DiPaolo/Sysco company in Columbus. In 1996, the DiPaolo family decided to get back into the independent foodservice business with a new name, RDP. The letters make sense if you know the name of Richie's children, Rita (Mizer), Dick and Paul. In addition to the brothers DiPaolo, several family members joined in, including grandsons Mark Mizer, Christopher DiPaolo and Rich DiPaolo III. The company continues to be successful to this day, with over forty employees and millions of dollars in annual sales. It still continues the DiPaolo tradition of being more than just a supplier by looking for innovations in the industry and consulting with customers, including pizzerias (of course), upscale restaurants, bars, ethnic eateries and the Columbus Zoo and Aquarium.

When Richie DiPaolo passed away, the community turned out to pay tribute to the man and family who made a difference in so many lives. Mark Mizer recalls that the manager at John Quint Funeral Home told him they had never had so many flowers delivered. Many people over the years have told him, "You don't know what Richie did for our family." Richie did a lot for Columbus pizzerias, creating a legacy that remains to this day.

ITALIAN AMERICAN NEIGHBORHOODS

Flytown, San Margarita, St. Clair Avenue, Marble Cliff, the "Bottoms" and Grandview were the neighborhoods where the majority of Italian American immigrants lived, worked and played. These tight-knit communities saw deep bonds of friendship and loyalty grow over the years between neighbors and extended family. Many of the early pizza shop owners grew up together in these neighborhoods and in some cases worked at a pizzeria together before opening businesses of their own. While the community is more dispersed today, the connections and memories are still strong. There were roughly one thousand Italians in Columbus at the dawn of the twentieth century. The numbers grew through the 1920s, and there was another migration in the 1950s and 1960s. In both eras, many of the immigrants came from the Abruzzo region of Italy.

Flytown

The rough borders of Flytown were the Olentangy River to the west, Goodale Street to Dennison Avenue to the east and the north Spruce Street to the south. The area served as home to many new immigrant arrivals, including Irish Americans, as well as African Americans. Italian Americans passed through as well. The area was home to the original TAT Ristorante. The name of the neighborhood has two stories. The first is that the area was growing so fast that houses just seemed to fly up. The second story suggests that the types of businesses in the area, as well as the density of residents, attracted large numbers of flies.

Grandview Heights

Grandview Heights was originally part of Marble Cliff. It became a separate village in 1906 and a city in 1931. While not thought of as an "Italian" village, the area had several streets dominated by multigenerational Italian families. Fred Lombardi at Panzera's Pizza grew up in and continued to live at a house on Westwood Avenue. The destination Italian restaurant in Columbus for many decades, Presutti's Villa, was located on West Fifth Avenue in Grandview.

Italian Village

The area is bounded by North High Street on the west, Fifth Avenue on the north, railroad tracks/North Fourth Street to the east and Interstate 670 on the south. Italian immigrants started to move to this area from Flytown in the 1890s. Italian craftsmen using stone from the nearby quarries created many of the buildings that still stand in the area today.

St. Clair Avenue

St. Clair Avenue featured four very active grocery stores, including DiPaolo Food Shoppe, which catered to the Italian American community during its heyday. Most residents left the area after World War II due to the construction of the freeway system and to flee to the suburbs. This is a section of the Milo area, which comprises Milo-Grogan.

San Margarita

At the beginning of the twentieth century, a few dozen Italian immigrant families settled along Trabue Road (between Hague Avenue and McKinley Avenue). These families pooled funds to help start St. Margaret of Cortona Catholic Church in 1921. The name of the area derives from the church. Most of the founding families have since left the area, but there are still traces of grapevines planted by residents over one hundred years ago.

Map showing key locations in Columbus pizza history. *Courtesy of Robert Patricy Creative.*

Marble Cliff

Founded in 1890 and then incorporated as the Hamlet of Marble Cliff in 1901, the name comes from the Marble Cliff Quarry Co., where many Italians worked.

The Bottoms

Also known as Franklinton or east Franklinton to some, it is so named because the area is below the water level of the nearby Scioto and Olentangy Rivers. The Bottoms is home to one of the oldest pizzerias in Columbus, Josie's.

4

PIZZA PROLIFERATES (1955-69)

By 1955, pizza was firmly established in Columbus culture. There were over fifty pizzerias in town and more in the offing. A certification for the importance of pizza as more than a cultural phenomenon was the 1955 phone book. For the first time, pizza had its own business listing. Pizzeria owners finally had an opportunity to easily advertise their businesses to newly prosperous households who were adding extra phones and second cars, making pizza even easier to pick up or deliver. No longer lost among the hundreds of restaurants listed together or filed under the bakery section in the phone book, pizza now had dedicated Yellow Pages section and was ready to turn on the heat in the restaurant industry.

LUIGI'S (1955)

Louis (Luigi) Tumeo opened the first pizzeria in Hilliard in 1955 at the corner of Cemetery Road and Main Street. In 1957, he moved the business just down Cemetery Road to the current location. Esther Lowry (Leeka) joined the business in the 1960s. Bev Leeka followed her mother's apron strings by joining in the 1970s. Continuing the family tradition, Bev's son Mike joined in the early 1980s. In 1984, the Leeka family purchased the pizzeria from their boss. They continued a tradition of community involvement and supporting local schools. The business was purchased from Mike and Denise Leeka in April 2019.

ANGE'S PIZZA (1957)

William "Ange" Strino Angeletti came to Columbus for a job at the Curtis Wright aircraft factory (later North American Aviation). He and his family settled on Cypress Avenue in Franklinton. In the early 1950s, Ange started a barbershop/sandwich shop on Fifth Avenue in a building he built himself. This location was very close to the original Tommy's Pizza. Tommy Iacono's pizzeria might have inspired Ange. We do know the two were friends and frequently golfed together. When Ange's family searched through old receipts from the barbershop, they found records that suggested he sold pepperoni or made sandwiches with pepperoni out of the shop.

The Angeletti family was displaced when the freeway cut into Franklinton, so Ange bought land in Whitehall and built his own pizza shop within fifty yards of their new house. The shop was opened in 1957. He obtained a liquor permit in the early 1960s but found that the shop was too close to Holy Spirit Catholic Church to allow him to sell alcohol and spirits when he wanted to.

There are countless stories that accumulate in a family business. One story shows the determination Ange had to serve his customers. An element common to all pizza shops is the heat from the oven. One day, Ange dropped a whole pizza on his leg. The heat was so intense that the skin of his leg fused with his pants. He kept working and finally went to the doctor two days later.

Steve Angeletti and Linda Hartman, longtime fixtures at Ange's, recall going on to the roof of the pizza shop to watch fireworks at the nearby park (what is today Norton Field Park).

There are countless special people involved with the shop over the years. John Porter was there from 1975 to 2019. Carl Childers is a someone many people have memories of. He worked there for decades. He had a wooden leg that Steve recalls knocking on to hear the sound. Carl had his leg amputated due an industrial accident in Kentucky. He started working at Ange's in the mid-1960s and retired in the early 1980s. After Ange passed away in 1972, Carl was the first non-family member to manage the pizza shop.

Ange's was one of the first businesses to deliver in the area, starting about 1978. The pizzeria started delivery due to competition from a newly opened Domino's location nearby. The family recalls that the Domino's lasted less than a year.

The family was also involved in some industry innovations. Ange's son William "Mike" Angeletti worked in the family pizza business most of his life. In 1984, he started Angeco to make insulated pizza boxes for delivery.

One page of pizza listings in Columbus Yellow Pages from 1959.

He was also very close with Bill Ezzo of the Ezzo Sausage Company. Many Columbus area pizzerias bought pepperoni from Patrick Cudahy Corporation (meat-packers). When the company moved from Wisconsin to Georgia, there were changes in products and pricing, so Mike (second generation) was among a handful of pizzeria owners who started working with the Ezzo Sausage Company to develop a new style of cupping pepperoni, which is extremely popular today.

In 2020, the Angeletti family continues the traditions of the family business. The original location at 139 South Yerling Street in Whitehall is still open, and over the decades, eight other locations have been added around central Ohio.

JOSIE'S PIZZA (1959)

The Catalfina family's journey to owning a pizzeria followed an unusual path. The surname was originally Catafamo but was changed to Catalfina at Ellis Island. Placid Catalfina found his way to Columbus, where he started working for the railroad. His coworkers could not pronounce *Placid*, so they started to call him Kelly. In time, he became known as Pa Kelly. Placid/Kelly bought a bar on West Broad Street, which he named Kelly's. In 1959, Placid and his wife, Josephine, purchased the former Caito's Pizza (952 West Broad Street), which was next door to the bar. It was named Josie's in honor of Josephine.

Placid's two sons, John and Anthony, worked in the family pizza business, and the two brothers and their wives purchased Josie's from their dad in the 1980s. John's wife, Joyce, had started working at Josie's in about 1962. In 1999, Anthony passed away, followed by his wife, Lois, a few months later. All of the Catalfina children (and many cousins) have worked at Josie's over the years. The business is very much a mom-and-pop shop, where many employees feel like family. Five employees have been there for over thirty years.

Josie's has changed a lot over the years. The Davis building has a history going back to 1900. Caito's Pizza was one of the earliest pizzerias in Columbus, so the Catalfinas had a good base to work with when they took over. The original layout of the space was set up as a diner, with low stools for eat-in customers and a soda fountain with ice cream service until the early 1960s.

Today, there are two Josie's locations. The original (952 West Broad Street) is often referred to as the "Bottoms" and the newer (3205 West Broad Street) location is referred to as the "Hilltop." Since both Josie's are on the same street, it is not uncommon for customers to drop in for pickup at the wrong location. A mural was painted on the wall at Josie's by third-generation pizza

Collection of old redemption cards at Josie's Pizza.

maker Jason. In the highly competitive pizza market where every penny counts, Josie's has retained a customer loyalty program for years that would cause most accountants to shake their heads. Customers are given a colored coupon/ticket on request when getting a pizza. If the customer turns in

49

ten, they receive a free pizza. Next to the mural on the wall is a glass case displaying an assortment of different colors and styles of pizza redemption coupons customers have turned in over the years.

TERITA'S PIZZA (1959)

Gus Iannarino started Terita's in April 1959, with the vision of a beer and wine carryout that also served food. Before opening, Gus was an insurance salesman who wanted to do something different. He had a cousin who ran a pizza place near the former Lockborune Air Force Base who provided advice and a good recipe for pizza dough. Originally, the menu included fried chicken, spaghetti, hamburgers, French fries and, of course, pizza, but as time went on, the menu shifted focus to pizza. The original location was near Twenty-Second Street and Cleveland Avenue before it moved to Mock Road and finally settled in at the current location on Cleveland Avenue in 1962. The name of the pizzeria is a derivative of the names of his first two children, Terry and Marita. They would one day work in the pizza shop along with their brothers, Mike and Tom.

When the business was started, Mrs. Iannarino thought Gus had a crazy idea, but relatives from both sides of the family pitched in to help the new business. A relative who was a butcher took a look at the sausage that was delivered to the shop and told Gus that he would be better off making his own. Terita's still makes its own sausage to this day. The mixer and other sausage making equipment date back one hundred years but still squeeze out a good product. Gus's dad and other family members worked shifts behind the counter, making meatballs and whatever else was needed to keep the business going and keep payroll down. Tom Iannarino started his career at Terita's in the fifth grade, working Fridays and Saturdays and all summer through high school. He kept helping at the shop while working as a firefighter but then took over day-to-day operations in 1982, before getting married.

While this is still a family business, many who work here feel like family. John Koontz used to live next door, so when he walked through the door the first time as a customer, he did not know he would still be doing so forty years later as a manager. Kyle Ray started in 1988. Jason Adkins has over twenty years behind the counter, and several others, including Donald McKelvey, have been at Terita's for just over or under twenty years.

There are a lot of loyal customers who have picked up their pizzas from Terita's for generations. One customer gave Gus a hand-drawn sketch of the iconic "pizza man" seen on all Terita's signs and menus. The origin story of the pizza man has been lost to time, but it probably began in the 1960s. Other customers miss the pizza so much that they have it shipped overnight to Florida. It is no small order to prep the pizzas to ship. Tom needs to prebake the dough/crust, pack in dry ice and ship it overnight. It is labor intensive and not cheap, but they are happy to do it for customers who can't find a good Columbus pizza down south.

A lot has changed since Terita's began. In the beginning, most of its refrigerated equipment was coin operated, so they needed to keep feeding their coolers loose change to use them. The company that owned them would come once per month to take the coins and service the machines. In the early days, Terita's offered delivery using a personal vehicle, but an employee got into a wreck, damaging three cars and creating a giant pile of bills for the attempted delivery of a fifty-cent sub. Gus swore then that he would take on a second or third job before he would consider offering delivery again, no matter what that meant to the business. The moratorium on the delivery option ended in 2018, when food delivery services started to court pizza shops, and while it is not the focus of the business, on a Friday night, a number of people are willing to pay to have their pizza delivered to them via a third party. All four of Gus's children worked in the pizzeria but only son Tom continues the second-generation legacy today.

Tom Iannarino cites several lessons his dad taught him over the years, which Tom feels have been the key to being open so long: "Treat the customer like gold" and "never cheapen the quality or you will hurt the business." A sign on the wall by the counter also spells out a longtime adage for the business: "If we please you, tell others. If not, tell us."

The Iannarino family has a long history in the Northland area, including strong ties to DeSales High School, which Tom and his children attended. The community can always count on Terita's to support a school team, area events and more.

On a slow day, guests might get lucky enough to see the ancient sausage-making equipment in the secondary prep area of Terita's. They still make their own sausage using grinders and other specialty items that are no longer sold. The sausage is unique. It is placed in long strips on pizzas and as thicker, long patties on the sausage sandwich that many customers love. It is a popular topping; Tom makes up to 150 pounds per week. Dough is made on-site using a stand mixer that dates to 1959.

EMELIO'S (1960)

Mike DiSabato was the founding father of the first family of central Ohio Wrestling. He was also one of the patriarchs of pizza in Columbus. When Mike opened Emelio's with his wife, Binnie, in 1960, the business became the vehicle to support Mike's wrestling habit. The Emelio's moniker came from the partner who helped start the business and who was later godfather to Mike and Binnie's son Leo. Emelio's has remained an institution on the west side. Even as the demographics of Georgesville Road have changed, the business has continued to draw in longtime customers from all over town.

When Emelio's started, the family lived nearby, which worked well for Mike and ensured a short commute to work for the rest of the family. Emelio's was a family business from day one. Mike ran the business as more of a club and bar. During the 1960s and 1970s, the west side was full of first-, second- and third-shift workers from GM and Westinghouse who were looking for a place to relax with food and drink before, maybe during and after work, and Emelio's was a favorite hangout.

Three generations of DiSabato's have worked at Emelio's. Mike (Papa) and Binne's (Nonna) workforce included many cousins, extended family and longtime friends. Many family members have been drafted to help out with last-minute rushes and large catering orders. Several of Mike and later Leo's high school wrestlers have worked (or trained) at Emelio's. Employees who are not family members are typically family friends. Bartender Jim Kennedy is a Saturday fixture known for being a great storyteller. Longtime employee and family friend Jimmy Gerst was referred to as the "seventh son" by Binnie and served as a pallbearer at Mike's funeral in 2002.

When Mike passed away, he left an incredible legacy for central Ohio Wrestling. His six sons won a combined eleven state titles at Ready High School from 1977 to 1991. His son Leo, who runs Emelio's today, won two of those titles. When Leo was growing up, part of his training was to run back and forth from the family home to the restaurant. Countless wrestlers were coached, mentored and supported in many ways. Binni's obituary asked friends to make contributions to Michael and Binnie DiSabato Family Athletic Scholarship Fund or the Team Davidson Wrestling Club (Hilliard Davidson High School).

Emelios's still caters for high school and Ohio State wrestling. Many of the photos on the wall are related to wrestling. Visitors will see plenty of posters supporting events and benefits for area Catholic schools, especially

Well-done pepperoni for the special salad at Emelio's Pizza.

Ready. Uncle Dom (Dominic DiSabato) does a wrestling benefit through Emelio's and was a wrestling coach at Hilliard Davidson High School.

Binnie made a lot of a changes after Mike died. She had always been active in the business, and she even designed one of the early logos. The original building was built by the Amicons, who are extended family. After Mike opened it in 1960, it was expanded three times and had a patio added by Binnie. She took over the reins after Mike passed away. She focused on transforming the space to more of a restaurant and less of a bar. She added paneling to the walls, as well as more framed photos and posters and other touches to spruce up the place.

Emelio's remains a gathering spot for family and friends today. It has a very active catering business. Longtime customers often order the "special salad" to go with their pizza. The special salad is actually pretty simple, but it features a generous pile of crisp, just shy of being burnt, cupped pepperoni. The house-made meatballs are also very popular as a side or on a perfectly baked sub. Snowbirds making their annual trip to Florida for the winter often take some half-baked Emelio's pizzas to sustain them.

PIZZA HOUSE (1961)

Cousins Bob Tiberi and Richie Dorn opened Pizza House at the northwest corner of the intersection of Lincoln Avenue and Sinclair Avenue in March 1961. The original location was mainly a carryout operation with seating for about twenty. The cousins used some of the same recipes passed down from their mothers. Billy Colasante was the first non-family employee. He started when he was fifteen years old. Colasante stayed with Pizza House for about fifteen years and then left to join his family bar business. Colasante never cut ties and continued to drop in for pizza over the years. In 1991, Pizza House moved to the current location in a former convenience store (once a Lawson's) at 747 Lincoln Avenue. The current location is about two hundred yards from the original but is much larger, with a full-size dining room and a dedicated pizza pick up area.

Colasante purchased the business in 1993 from Bob and Richie. Many employees have worked at the Pizza House for three or more decades (including Jeff Tiberi and Doug Wilford), a rare thing in any business.

Extreme Pepperoni Pizza at Vick's Gourmet Pizzeria.

Many members of Colasante's family have worked in the business over the years. The familiar faces among the staff working in the house gives the restaurant a friendly, family feeling. The interior is lined with local little league trophies accumulated from years of supporting teams in the area. Also lining the walls are a multitude of media stories collected over the years and many awards from contests, including the Slice of Clintonville. Pizza House consistently landed in the top twenty-five pizza places in numerous polls and best-of lists over the decades. While pizza remains the focus of the business, there is a deep menu of other Italian fare (including the author's favorite, an open meatball sandwich). In 2017, Colasante's son, Rodd Carmean, bought Pizza House from his father. Rodd worked at both the original and current location while growing up, so he knew the family business well.

VICK'S (1961)

Hollis and Louise Vickers transformed a former dry goods store on Main Street in Reynoldsburg into Vick's Pizza in 1961. It was not an ideal space—seating was limited, and pickup could be a challenge during peak times—but it quickly became a favorite in the community. The two had previous experience at 3C Pizza in 1958 (later a Cy's Pizza). In 1978, their son Doug and his wife, Charlotte, took over the reins of the business. In 2013, their neighbor Connell Hardware closed two storefronts down the block. Connell's had been a fixture on Main Street since 1872. Doug and Charlotte knew the building would be a lot of work, but the chance of a larger space was hard to ignore. Encouragement from the community with a desire to keep the block vibrant tipped the scale, resulting in Vick's Gourmet Pizzeria opening at 7345 East Main Street in 2017. The addition of a larger kitchen, plenty of seating and an expanding menu made Vick's more popular than ever.

Vick's is known for its slow-cooked signature sauce, which is a blend of oregano, basil, garlic, parmesan cheese and two different types of tomatoes. In addition to pizza, a longtime favorite is the meatball sub featuring plenty of sauce and weighty meatballs with thick and dense cheese with just a trace of char on the edges. The sturdy bun can withstand the mass of meatballs and sauce. The sub buns are shipped in from a highly respected bakery in Pittsburgh. The meatballs contain applesauce for moistness, and the sauce is cooked with the sausage.

The interior of the restaurant blends the 1872 brick walls and old photographs with modern wood and plenty of TVs. The new space allowed the addition of a patio and designated carryout space, so there is something to please everyone.

MASSEY'S 2.0 (1962)

Guido Casa was no greenhorn to the pizza business. He was one of the owners of Chef Cassino, which was among the first pizzerias in Columbus. Chef Cassino was one of the busiest too. Paul and Dick DiPaolo recall that the business ordered more food than anyone else, usually twenty-five to thirty cases of supplies each week. They could recall this because it was their job to load, and each case was sixty-four pounds. Guido Casa was also a partner in Riccardi's Restaurant in Beechwold, which offered pizza with an array of other items. He sold his part of the restaurant to Eugene Riccardi to buy Massey's Pizza in 1962.

Guido grew up in Flytown and might have made pizza as early as 1948 at Anton's Restaurant in Worthington. Many referred to Guido as the

Interior of Vick's Gourmet Pizzeria. The building dates to 1872.

Godfather of Columbus Pizza. He was well known and respected by his pizza peers and a frequent golf partner for many of them. At Massey's, Casa worked on perfecting the dough recipe, which uses specially ground cornmeal. He also laid the foundation for what would become known as Guido brand pepperoni. As oven technology was starting to shift to conveyor ovens, he became associated with the phrase "you can't fake the bake, chain conveyors are for auto parts not for cooking pizzas," which is still on Massey's website today.

Casa encouraged many people to get into the pizza business and strongly promoted pizza in general and Massey's throughout Columbus. Massey's has billed itself as the Cadillac of pizzas, which might have been related to Casa's trademark gold Cadillac with the family emblem prominently displayed. Many employees recall Casa's number one rule for the company: "Don't Compromise Price for Quality."

DONATOS (1963)

If you live in Columbus, you have heard of Donatos Pizza. Many people throughout Ohio and nine other states have eaten a pizza from one of many locations. But it took a long time to grow to more than one pizzeria. The roots of Donatos go back to the mid-1950s. Jim Grote started working at Cy's Pizza (corner of Deshler and Parsons Avenues) when he was thirteen. The two owners were Hollis and Cy. Hollis had a strong influence on Grote. Because he was such a good employee and passionate about the business, the owners offered to sell the pizzeria to him when he was a sophomore in high school. The terms were good. He would have five years to pay off the balance owed, and current revenues would allow him to meet the schedule and cover operating costs. Grote sought the counsel of his father and a favor. He was hoping for a small loan and for someone to cover for him on Fridays until football season was over. His dad quickly said no. To him, pizza was a fad and would not get his son anywhere. He should finish high school and then go to college and get a degree. Grote listened to his father's advice but kept working at the pizzeria after it changed hands.

Grote attended Ohio State University after high school, but still had the business of pizza on his mind. In the summer of 1963, Grote dropped out of school to buy Donatos Pizza from Don Potts. He asked for a loan totaling $1,300 from his dad and his future father-in-law. Don Potts had created the name Donatos, which he loosely translated from Latin as "to give a good thing." Potts figured Donatos was a much better name for a pizza place than Potts Pizza. Grote thought the same, as Grote Pizza Pie was not going to fly.

They moved the equipment from the former Donatos to a storeroom in front of Baumann's plumbing shop (Grote's father-in-law's shop). Family and friends helped him do all of the buildout, including the plumbing. He just had to pay for the vent pipe. Grote's mother made the dough. Both parents made sausage and meatballs. The new Donatos had a busy first day due to a twenty-five-cents-off coupon in the newspaper, which created a line almost a block long before opening at 5:00 p.m.

Not too long after, the business moved across the street (to 1000 Thurman Avenue) and built a building out of black bricks (from London, Ohio) and bought the house behind it, where the Grotes to lived. This Donatos did not have a waiting area, so if pizza was not ready, guests would wait at the Grotes' house. Employees would write B.A.G. on the order, translated as Back at Grotes'.

Grote opened two more stores in the late 1960s but closed them after a short period of time. He decided he would not open any additional pizzerias until he had all of the processes in place to guarantee consistency and his high standard of service. It would take several years to get there, but few have dedicated as much effort to ensure that a pizza consistently meets a defined standard as Jim Grote.

ZAMARELLI'S PIZZA PALACE (1963)

Zam's, Zammy's or Zammies, as locals call Zamarelli's Pizza Palace, has been a fixture on Front Street in Grove City since 1963. Opened and operated by Andy Zamarelli, the business changed very little from opening day to today. Zamarelli was as well known, if not more so, for his community involvement. He was a member of many local organizations, including the Jaycees and Knights of Columbus. He was voted Man of the Year in Grove City in 1976 and 1980. He and his wife, Catherine "Katie" (Mollica) Zamarelli, opened Mama Lucia's Restaurant in Hilliard before the launch of the pizza business. Kate was well known for her work on behalf of many local charities, especially for people with developmental disabilities. Andy passed away in 1995 and Katie in 2016. Relative Jack Middendorf and his wife, Tina, run the business today.

Panzera's (1964)

The origin of Panzera's Pizza reads a lot like a Horatio Agler rags-to-riches tale. The Panzera family immigrated to the Grandview area in 1955, just before Nick Panzera observed his fifth birthday. They arrived from the Abruzzo/Abruzzi section of Italy, speaking little English, and immediately set themselves to work. Nick started working at Tedeschi Italian Bakery (at Third and Doten Avenues) in Grandview. Initially, he was bagging bread, but over time, he took on many other roles. Nick and some of his brothers would sometimes work at nearby Leonardo's Pizza, as well. When Nick was twelve, Tedeschi Bakery closed, so he was out of a job. In late 1964, Nick and his brother Phillip, with the help of many family members, decided to run the bakery space as a pizzeria and called it Panzera's. It was a small operation, open seven days per week, with one oven and dough mixed by hand. And it was managed and operated by thirteen-year-old Nick Panzera.

One of the keys to making this work was Nick's teacher George Sotiris Georgas. As Nick was getting ready to open the pizzeria, George kept asking him questions about what items would be on the menu and how much Nick was planning to charge for each specialty offered. Nick was surprised by a stack of menus given to him by George, who made them on the school's mimeograph machine as a surprise for opening day. George also knew that Nick was working late nights at the pizzeria, so he arranged for Nick to have a "job" in the school book room, which allowed Nick to sleep and/or study the first two periods of the day. The first five-dollar sale at Panzera's Pizza was from George, and it was framed on the wall for years.

In 1966, older brother and business partner Phillip was working at the nearby quarry, but it was laying off employees. He came to Nick and said, "I'm moving." Since he had just moved to a new house, Nick was confused and asked Phillip why he would move again so soon. Phillip explained that he was not moving to another house—he was moving to California to find work. At this point, Nick was fifteen and in high school and didn't feel he could run the business on his own. He considered putting the business up for sale, but after a less-than-desirable offer, he decided to figure out how to make it work. He decided he would start advertising but knew that before he could start marketing the business, he needed to upgrade everything in the pizzeria to increase his production volume. Nick worked with Stan Becker, a salesman at Wasserstrom, to order $10,000 of equipment, including another oven, a mixer, a slicer, a double-door refrigerator, pots and pans—everything needed to allow a few people to make more pizzas in less time. The price tag for these upgrades was high, so an owner was needed to sign on the bottom line. Nick was fifteen, and Stan told him he was too young to sign the contract. Nick replied to Becker that his dad would sign it, but Stan knew that his dad did not speak English. So, Nick countered that he would read the contract to his dad. Stan was a bit wary of that. In the end, Nick signed the contract with his dad's name while Stan looked the other way.

After the new equipment was in place, Nick worked with a customer to print ten thousand menus, including coupons. Then Nick loaded up a car to drive his nieces and nephews around the Grandview neighborhoods, dropping them off at one end of the block and picking them up at the other side, to deliver fliers throughout the area. People started calling in orders and dropping in the first day of flier delivery, leading to some very busy days. Phillip came home to visit shortly thereafter and was amazed at the stacks of pizzas waiting to be picked up in the shop.

Nick got married in 1969. He started buying rental properties in the area to diversify his income. Many of the pizzeria's customers were police officers, and they would often say, "Nick you should be a cop," so when Nick turned twenty-one (1972), he applied for the police academy and was accepted. Eventually, Nick's wife told him he had to give up at least one business, so he decided to sell the shop to Fred Lombardi and his wife (Nick's sister) in 1976. Fred had worked at Panzera's (and Leonardo's Pizza) for years, including managing the shop since Nick started working as a police officer. Nick was once called to Panzera's Pizza in response to a robbery call; items stolen included the framed dollar bill from the first sale.

Panzera's Pizza moved a few times since opening in 1964, and in 1983, Fred Lombardi moved the shop to the present location at Grandview and Third Avenues. Today, Fred is "retired," which seems to mean he is working what most would consider a normal workweek. Fred remains a fixture in the kitchen, making dough and sauce and prepping pizzas. Many members of the extended family have worked at the shop over the decades. The recipes are all Panzera family recipes, with no changes since 1964. None of the recipes are written down; all are passed along by one person showing and expecting the other person to continue doing the same. Panzera's still makes its dough, pizza sauce, spaghetti sauce and many other Italian specialties from scratch. Fred passed the pizza peel of day-to-day operations to his son Carlo many years ago, and today, guests can often find Fred, Carlo and (grandson) Andy kneading and tossing the dough behind the counter.

A non-pizza menu item that has been popular since the 1980s is the Monster Sub, which is a fusion of an Italian and meatball sub wedded between two buns. Another thing that customers can count on at Panzera's is Nick dropping in several times per week (when he is not visiting brother Paul at Paul's Pantry just around the corner). You will find a lot of important things at Panzera's that are not on the menu: three generations of family who are proud of their pizza and connected to their neighborhood and their customers in a way that few businesses can compete against. All of this because a thirteen-year-old needed a job and the extended Panzera/Lombardi family always helped each other out to keep the family business going. That alone is worth a visit—the pizza is a bonus.

Historical Side Dish

Phillip Panzera came home from California to visit the pizzeria shortly after Nick expanded the kitchen operation and started his marketing blitz. While Phillip was walking in, he noticed a man walking out of the nearby insurance agency, which was a new neighbor. At the same time, the insurance agent in question did a double take, noticing Phillip as well. Each sensed that they knew the other, and after a lot of conversational sleuthing, they figured out that they had met in Italy during World War II (over twenty years before) when the jeep the insurance agent was riding in picked up a hitchhiking Phillip on a dirt road.

PAPA JOE'S (1964)

Papa Joe's was opened by brothers Don and Jerry Parker in 1964 on Lockbourne Road, not far from their house. The name comes from a Pat Boone song of the era, "Wang Dang Taffy-Apple Tango." In 1970, they opened a location on the Ohio State University campus at 1573 North High Street. More of a bar than a pizza place, the campus Papa Joe's sold beer in buckets—not bottles of beer in buckets, but just beer in buckets. When Papa Joe's and nearby business burned down on April 3, 1996, it marked the beginning of a slightly more temperate student body. Jerry Parker grew Papa Joe's to over fifteen locations. At one point, Papa Joes was reported to sell more draft beer than any other business in the country. Today, there are still several Papa Joe's locations in central Ohio. Parker died in 1992, but family members still own the business, and many locations are owned by former employees.

MINELLI'S PIZZA (1967)

The original Minelli's pizza opened at 3858 Sullivant Avenue in 1967. Prior to being a Minelli's, the spot was a very successful pizza location for TAT. The 1956 oven at this Minelli's was inherited from TAT, which had acquired the oven from a bankruptcy sale of Jimmy Massey's Drive in Pizzeria. The oven remained in use until the Sullivant location closed in December 2019.

Bob Minshall and Guy Ferrelli opened the pizzeria and fused their surnames together to create the name of the business (Min-elli's). The Ferrelli family took over ownership of the business. Guy's daughter Jill ran

Jeff Thompson at Lincoln Village Joseppi's, showing the twenty-eight-inch pizza crust for the Mega Meat Challenge.

the Sullivant Road location. His son Jeff runs the Wilson Road location today. He grew up in the family business, lived on the west side and at one time worked at the Delphi plant, which brought much business and prosperity to the area before it closed.

The Wilson Road location hosts Columbus Police Academy recruits twice per year for mock crime scene scenarios. Customers or passersby can participate in training future police officer—not in eating pizza but in how to deal with hostage situations or robberies in progress.

Customers at the Wilson Road location might get befuddled by the speed of service at Minelli's, until they realize that Jeff's twin daughters, Kaci and Kelli, work there together. Business is brisk at the Wilson Road location, but many note that it is hard to replicate the atmosphere and the *je ne sais que* of pizza from a sixty-year-old oven at the Sullivant Avenue Minelli's.

Joseppi's (1969)

Robert (Bob) Thompson opened Joseppi's in 1969. He invested so much time in the business that he put a bed in the back room. Robert taught his son Chuck how to make a pizza when he was only four years old. Robert was well known for his generosity to the community, especially toward young children. He always made sure they had a penny for the gumball machine. Robert's other passion was motorcycles. Unfortunately, he and his wife were killed in a motorcycle accident in May 1998.

It had always been the plan for Chuck to take over the restaurant when his father retired, and the unexpected passing of his father advanced the handoff. Chuck sold his trucking business so that he could devote all of his effort to the two Joseppi's Pizzas he inherited.

Soon after taking over, Chuck entered the 1999 Columbus Pizza Challenge and came in first place in all three categories—a first in the history of the event. This earned the business a lot of attention and an article in the December 1999 issue of *Pizza Today*. Sadly, Chuck died in June 2018.

Today, family members operate the four Joseppi's locations in central Ohio. They maintain the traditions and recipes of their predecessors, but each location has some unique aspects to its operations. The Sullivant Road location has a great tradition. Since 2013, it has closed for Memorial Day in honor of Robert and all staff, with a spouse or plus one and kids, go by bus to Kings Island or Cedar Point for the day. The current owner took over the business when Bob died because he did not want a non-family member to buy it. Before he purchased, he came in every day for a month to eat pizza with his son to ensure it was right and to make sure taking over the business was right for them. They could earn more money doing something else, but they enjoy coaching employees and creating opportunities and jobs in the neighborhood.

At the Lincoln Village location, owner Jeff Thompson is a grandson of Robert. He started working at the family pizzeria when he was twelve. His location offers the Topper, the signature pizza for Joseppi's. It is piled high with plenty of pepperoni on top of provolone and grated parmesan cheese. What Thompson has that the other locations don't is the Mega Meat Challenge. This is a twenty-eight-inch diameter pizza, and when cut (in squares, of course), there are about fifty-eight slices. It takes thirty minutes to prepare the pizza and two people to transport it. It must be ordered with advance notice, but it will not be started until both contestants are on-site. Jeff shared that, on several occasions, he has had people (scoundrels) order the pizza and not show up. Considering the time, effort and cash that goes into creating this megalith, that is too much to lose.

The ingredients for this pizza pile up over an inch thick and include layers of Topper pepperoni (made for the Topper pizza, this is the old-school, crisp at the edges pepperoni that is harder to find in the pizza biz today), Italian sausage, ham, ground beef and bacon.

These are the rules for competing in the Mega Meat Challenge:

- The team of two sits at the round table near the counter so they can be monitored the whole time.
- Stay near the table at all times—they can get up to do a lap around the table, stretch or get more pop from the soda fountain.
- They may not go to the bathroom or leave the building.
- They have sixty minutes to consume the entire pizza (no knocking meat on the ground or under the table).
- Buckets are provided in case one or both lose intestinal integrity. (No one has used these to date.)
- Dipping sauces (ranch and hot sauce) are provided on request to help slide the slices down the hatch.
- No one is allowed to sit with contestants at the table or approach when the mega meat eaters are in competition mode.
- The challenge can only be attempted Monday to Thursday from 4:00 to 9:00 p.m.

Rules for the Mega Meat Challenge. (The author was defeated.)

Winning the challenge offers more than just a boost to self-esteem. The winners get $100 in cash, $150 in Joseppi's gift cards, two T-shirts and their photo on the wall. That is well worth an hour of your time. The cost of losing is $50. Only one team has completed the challenge. If you don't finish, you will have plenty of leftovers for days.

BAKERS BEHIND THE
PIZZA MAKERS—AUDDINO'S BAKERY

Michael and Rosa Auddino grew up in the same village in Italy and were friends growing up. Their families left Italy for new opportunities for their children. Rosa came to Columbus via Ellis Island. Michael headed to Germany, where he eventually became a baker. He then moved to Canada and was reconnected with Rosa through family connections. The two courted, and he moved to Columbus after they were married. During their dating days, they would often meet at the Linden Bakery. They became friends with the owner. In 1965, he was ill and offered the bakery to the

The deck oven at Emelio's Pizza.

couple. Michael did not have enough capital to buy the business. Rosa was able to get a loan for $500 and purchased the business for Michael. The two started working seven days a week at their Cleveland Avenue bakery. As they added children to the family, the children started spending most of their time at the bakery as well. They were at the Cleveland Avenue location for a few years before they moved Auddino's Bakery to the current location on Clara Avenue. Since then, the family has supplied bread, rolls, pizza crusts, desserts and more to restaurants in central Ohio. If you have eaten at an Italian restaurant, a pizza place or even an American restaurant in the area, there is a good chance you have eaten many things from Auddino's.

The bakery does have a walk-in shop where anyone can come to buy bread or harder-to-find Italian ingredients. A bonus is access to house-made cannoli and donuts, including the almost legendary dousant, the forbearer of the legendary cronut (a croissant in donut form). You can also expect interesting commentary from any of the family members covering the counter between their duties for the day. Although Auddino's does not serve pizza, the bakery supports many of the pizza shops throughout the city. Their sons, Rosario (Roy), Dante and Marco, as well as the third generation, continue to bake away.

Ovens

The first pizza ovens were open hearths. For centuries, wood and coal fired brick ovens were the way to make pizza. Some pizza makers used pans and conventional ovens in a pinch in the 1930s and 1940s. The first major innovation in oven technology was in 1945, when Ira Nevin of the Bronx manufactured Bakers Pride Gas Fired Ovens. These ovens were reasonably priced, produced a good heat for pizza and were versatile enough to cook subs and other items. These ovens helped fuel the growth of pizzerias.

Pizza oven options evolved quickly as pizza took off in the 1950s. As pizzerias became busier, the need to peel out pizzas quickly and consistently became even more important. Early pizza shops were happy to get deck ovens in the 1950s, which would allow them to cook multiple pies at once. The downside was that they required a lot of skill to monitor the different cook times, depending on ingredients and the location of certain sweet spots in the oven. Pizzas cooked in these ovens must be constantly monitored by a pie slinger. As the 1960s progressed, more pizzerias were switching to conveyor and convection ovens. Guido Casa of Massey's preferred the open flame deck ovens so that the crispness of the crust could be varied to customer preference.

Each oven has pros and cons, depending on the type of pizza being made. Conveyor ovens provide consistency. The pizza is dropped onto the rolling conveyor to be heated at progressively changing but consistent temperatures from start to finish. These ovens require little training, and the operator can do other things while the pizza cooks.

Convection ovens are sometimes used for smaller operations, like bars or fast-service establishments. They cannot do the volume of a deck oven but can heat or reheat premade products and take up less space. The type of oven a pizza place chooses depends on many factors, including budget, available space, how much the business is able to train staff and the type of pizza that will be made. Many longtime pizza makers swear that the older the oven the better the pizza.

5

PIZZA PREEMINENCE (1970-84)

Today about 50 percent of pizzerias are national or regional chains. In this golden age of Columbus pizza, the beginning of the pizza wars saw many chains looking to establish a foothold in the Columbus market. Pizza Hut and Domino's were early entries, establishing a handful of locations in the late 1960s. For the most part, mom-and-pop pizzerias held their own and thrived in spite of the ability of chains to saturate markets with free delivery, lower prices and an escalation of coupons. Columbus has always loved pizza, and in this era, the growth of independent pizzerias made it the preeminent food in a city that was often called the fast-food capital of the nation. The period from 1970 to 1984 saw a rapid growth in pizza throughout the city, including many chains aggressively expanding into Columbus to get their slice of a hot market and because the city is a national test bed for new restaurant concepts and chains that want to expand. If you can make it in Columbus, you have a good chance of making it anywhere.

D&EZO's (1970)

D&EZO's pizza opened in 1970. According to current owner Greg Stanley, the D stands for "Dad" the E stands for "Evan" and ZO just sounds Italian. The Westlake family created the name and ran the business until Stanley

Exterior of D&EZO's Pizza on the south side.

took over the south side establishment in 2000. The two-story building is located on Brown Road and was frequented by many truck drivers working for Roadway. They liked a hearty meal, so the Roadway Monster sub was created for them. It is an Italian sub with meatballs, mushrooms, spaghetti sauce and extra cheese added. The pizzeria also features larger than normal pizzas. D&EZO's serves a seventeen-inch pizza (family sized or extra-large) and a thirty-inch pizza known as the Destroyer. The pizzeria remains a south side favorite, and many former customers are happy to make the trek back to fill up on pizza. While not well known outside of the south side, the pizza did get a burst of attention after winning the 1995 Columbus Pizza Challenge.

EAGLES VILLA (1971)

Eagles Pizza was purchased by the Keesee family in 1971. The pizzeria was started by the Marna Seunm family in the 1960s under the name New Albany Pizza. The second owner, Bob Dickendasher, changed the name to

Eagles Pizza in honor of the New Albany High School mascot. In 1972, the Keese's moved the business to the present location. In 1973, the family purchased a pizzeria in Johnstown, which they called Johnnies Villa Pizza. They added Villa to the Eagles name to link the businesses.

The Keesee and Doran families have a long history in New Albany. Several of the family members are also hardcore history buffs. Dennis Keesee has a focus on Civil War and World War II history. In addition to presentations on the subject, Dennis wrote the book *Too Young to Die: Boy Soldiers of the Union Army 1861–1865* in 2001. Forefather James Doran settled in the area after the Revolutionary War. Tom Keesee married Marjorie Doran, and they built their house on part of the old family farm. Tom remodeled a former grocery store with origins in 1858 into Eagles Villa Pizza in 1972. The family added other heirlooms to the interior of the pizzeria, including photos of New Albany's past and the oxen yoke James Doran used. The Eagles Villa hosts the website New Albany Stories, which shares area events and history.

While history is a passion of the family, it does not mean their pizza choices are a throwback to the 1950s or earlier. The menu sports many modern pizza choices, including taco pizza and chicken bacon BBQ. The dessert menu does have one throwback to the past: cakes from Resch's Bakery (on the east side of Columbus since 1912) have been featured for years.

Eagles Villa is the quintessential New Albany hangout. Many New Albany teenagers had their first job here. As New Albany continues to grow, Eagles Villa keeps the community rooted in the past.

MASSEY'S PIZZA 3.0 (1972–1984)

Phillip Casa started working at Massey's at the age of thirteen in 1962, when his dad took over the business. In 1972, Guido Casa turned over the keys of Massey's to his son. Guido remained a fixture at Massey's until he passed away in 1976. Phillip worked to expand Massey's locations in central Ohio. Massey's held on to traditions longer than most other spots in town. Guido's brother Joe worked at Falters Meats, which supplied the meat for Massey's sausage until about 1990. Massey's kept serving carryout pizzas in signature brown paper sleeves/tents instead of boxes longer than most other places. (Boxes of the era steamed up the pizza, and the Casas would not stand for that.) Massey's also held on to what some call traditional cut—straight down the middle long pieces, which can still be sliced on request to old-school customers.

Massey's had some incredible employees during this era. In 1977, Randy Hicks started working at Massey's Pizza on his sixteenth birthday. A friend at school had a locker near him and asked if he was getting a job when football season was over. The friend said he had started working at Massey's. Randy recognized that it was his uncle's business. Randy started to work with his uncle Guido and cousin Philip and, over the years, worked every job Massey's had to offer. He purchased the Reynoldsburg Massey's from Phillip in 1996. He sold it in 2004 but could not stay away from the business for long; he was back to work after a year.

Longtime customers of the Whitehall Massey's still ask about the twins Marc Runck and Clark Runck, who were fixtures for years. The twins enjoyed getting customers mixed up on who was who at the shop. Clark was a thirty-eight-year employee at Massey's. He started as a pizza maker and ended his career as president. He was called "Mr. Massey's Pizza" and was inducted as the first employee to the Massey's Pizza Hall of Fame.

DANTE'S (1973)

Joe Apollonio immigrated to Columbus from the Abruzzo region of Italy at age fourteen. He spoke little English and settled with relatives in Grandview. He started working and going to school as soon as he arrived. His first job was as a dishwasher at Romeo's Pizza (Fifth and North Star), which was the first pizzeria in Columbus. He worked with Romeo Sirij, one of the founders, who helped with his foundation in the restaurant business. A friend from school, Paul Panzera, told him about an opening at Leonardo's Pizza, so he started working there (the original location at West First Avenue in Grandview). As Joe's English language skills improved, he was asked to be a manager at the Worthington Leonardo's and the Kenny Road Leonardo's.

As he was starting a new family, he needed more income and wanted more control over his work hours, so by pooling funds from his brother, sister and other family members, he started Dante's Pizza in March 1973. The location was home to several restaurants over the years, including a place called Sandy's. The previous business had some struggles, so he knew he would need a different name and would need to very quickly establish the quality of his menu. He named the restaurant after his brother. At the start, most of the employees were family members, including his niece Tizianna, who now owns Enrico's pizza. Many of the employees feel like family, with at least two, Shirley and Pat, there for over thirty years. Little has changed since Dante's opened in 1973. Transactions are still cash and check only. The decor and layout are functional. Pickup customers can watch their pizzas being assembled and cooked through the glass counter. Dine-in guests have about a dozen four-top tables to choose from, and it is not uncommon for all or most of them to get pushed together to serve a soccer team or large family.

The pizza dough is made fresh daily. The pizza, spaghetti sauces, signature Italian dressing and many other items are made in house. The sausage is made locally with a recipe Joe has used for decades and is a favorite topping for longtime customers. After two heart attacks and open-heart surgery, Joe is still coming in early to prep the business for the day, make sauces and dough and deal with deliveries, but he is typically gone before the first customers come through the door. As is the case for most old-school pizza shop owners, Joe was a regular at the American Italian Golf Club at the (now closed) Riviera Country Club and regularly played with the Gattos, who own a nearby pizzeria. Joe enjoys seeing several generations of Clintonville families returning year after year and watching kids become adult customers who bring in their own children. Joe foresees no changes at Dante's. It will remain a cash business. Additional traffic from delivery services is too complicated to consider for this small pizzeria with the corner spot in a busy shopping plaza. Dante's will remain a time capsule of the 1970s, and that is the way everyone likes it.

Rotolo's (1974)

Luigi and Mafalda Rotolo were first-generation Italian immigrants hailing from the Abruzzi region of Italy. They grew up in the same village, Cerreto, near Naples. Mafalda's path to Columbus was via New York City, while Luigi immigrated to Canada. The two married in Canada and then moved to Grandview in 1963.

Luigi worked construction jobs, and Mafalda worked at a series of restaurants, including Romeo's Pizza, Prescutti's Villa and Casa di Pasta. The two are related by blood, marriage or godparentage to a host of Italian restaurant owners in Columbus, including the owners of LaScala, DaVinci's, Milanosa and Monte Carlo. Malfada is a cousin of Joe Appolino at Dante's Pizza.

The Rotolo family lived on Westwood Avenue in Grandview. Their yard connected to the lot that was then the home to Kings Carry Out. They bought the business when the owner died and ran it as a carryout for a year. In 1974, they tore down the building to build Rotolo's Pizza. Luigi did all of the interior construction. The spot was quickly a neighborhood favorite, serving some customers two to three meals per week, since they offered much more than pizza. Rotolo's was open late-night hours, much to the chagrin of a teenage Dominic "Dom" Rotolo, who lamented that the walk from their house to the pizzeria was the "shortest, longest walk of my life." Teenage Dom often worked well past 2:00 a.m. on weekends, while his friends were out having fun. Rotolo's quickly started making best-of lists, including some national exposure.

Rotolo's Pizzeria has been a family affair since the day the doors opened and even more so when Luigi died of a heart attack after shoveling snow from the restaurant sidewalk. Mafalda and the Rotolo children, Dominic, Marisa (Mentel) and Rina, have continued the legacy of the original Rotolo's. In 2002, Rotolo's entered a partnership with Kroger and four independent grocery stores to supply take-and-bake pizza. The project grew faster than they could keep up with, but it was a good product with a good run. In 2004, the Rotolos expanded with two more locations, followed by two more in 2005. The family found that the challenge of staffing, ensuring consistency and other logistics made the expansion a headache and took the family element out of the business. Today, they are back to one location and a short commute to work.

The Rotolo's on West Fifth Avenue has changed little since opening in 1974. Dominic continues his father's tradition of working construction during the day and making pizza at night. Third generation Rotolos have served their time as well, minus the late-night shifts of their parents.

LITTLE SICILY'S (1975)

Thomas Leitch and C.J. Mazza opened Little Sicily's on Brice Road in 1975. The spot was mainly a carryout but quickly earned a loyal following. The motto for the business is "Pizza Worth the Drive," and many customers do drive thirty minutes or more to get their pizza fix. One of those longtime customers, Tim Bucco, started eating pizza there when he was going to Groveport High School shortly after Little Sicily's opened. In 2006, Bucco and his wife, LuAnne, purchased their favorite pizza place. The two ate there when they were dating and became good friends with the owner. When the shop opened, it had seating for only a dozen or so. The restaurant expanded to a capacity of about seventy in the 1990s, and when the Buccos took over, they added a patio to seat about fifty in good weather. The patio also allowed them to add bands and other live entertainment for the weekends.

The interior is very sports focused, with a plentitude of Ohio State University football and local high school sports memorabilia on the walls. The restaurant also hosts its own fantasy football league. The pizza is still made in brick ovens using the original dough recipe from day one. The only big change to the menu from the Buccos is the house-made lasagna, which is a meat lover's delight. Little Sicily is classic Columbus-style pizza with generous toppings. A longtime favorite is the Ziggy Special Pizza, featuring Italian sausage and sauerkraut. Another popular combination is Joe's Special Pizza, with pepperoni, chopped jalapeños, hot peppers, onions and light extra cheese.

The pizzeria does a lot to support local high schools, sponsoring car washes and donating gift certificates. The staff is very tight knit and considered part of the family by the Buccos, to the point that Tim often says, "Let our family serve your family."

FLYERS PIZZA (1976)

In 1972, Wayne Ulrey's wife, Esther, died, leaving him to raise their four sons alone. In 1976, after his twenty-plus years working for Westinghouse on the city's west side, the plant closed, and Ulrey needed a new direction. Although he had no experience in the pizza business, he purchased a small pizzeria called Tonni's in West Jefferson. Legend has it that he was sold the business on the hope that the seller could buy the business back at a bargain price when Ulrey would, no doubt, fail later. Wayne paused on the purchase of the business for a month to wait for his son Mark to turn sixteen so that he could be a delivery driver. Mark reports that he had his share of accidents learning the delivery business. On the first day, the pizzeria made $173. Despite of his lack of experience, Wayne made it past the first week, and the business continued to grow. It was very much a family business, and there were cots in the back room so that Ulrey could watch his sons while he worked nights.

In 1979, the family bought a doughnut shop on West Main Street in West Jefferson, replacing it with a pizza shop later. They opened a second location on Norton Road in 1987 (and moved it in 2002). When the third shop opened in 1992 in Hilliard, they changed the name of the company to Flyers Pizza. The next location was in Grove City in 2002. Additional locations popped up in Powell, Blacklick, Groveport and a second in Grove City, for a total of eight pizzerias.

Although Wayne has retired from the business, his sons, Mark, Dave, Scott and Steve, and daughter, Linda, are very active in managing the company today. They have continued the tradition of sourcing their cheese from award-winning Foremost Farms in Wisconsin.

CAPUANO'S (1977)

In 1977, Joe Flegle bought Capuano's Pizza in Pataskala from owner Joe Capuano. Flegle was no stranger to pizza. In the 1960s, when he was sixteen years old, he started working for Guido and Phillip Casa at Massey's Pizza. He stayed for six years. Guido Casa worked with Joe to teach him how to make dough, and soon, he became a dough specialist. He advanced to manager of the Whiteball Massey's location. In 1974, he moved to Pataskala. After starting the pizzeria, he met his wife, Lana, just before the blizzard of 1978. Joe received a lot of support from his mother and father over the years to grow the business. Initially, Capuano's was more of a hang out, but together the family turned it into a family-friendly spot. The Flegle children worked in the pizzeria while growing up, and the grandchildren might follow the tradition. Flegle's employees included several families, with two generations of service to the business. Joe has watched several families grow up visiting the pizzeria. He has stated that he will retire when a third-generation employee starts working there.

Flege insists on continuing to use the finest and freshest ingredients. Dough is made fresh daily from his own secret recipe, and pizzas are cooked in an aged brick oven to achieve the consistency he wants. Phillip Casa has commented on Facebook about the quality of the Massey's alumni, stating that Capuano's is among the best pizzas in central Ohio.

Pizza at Iacono's on Kenny Road.

IACONO'S (1978)

Stephen "Steve" Iacono grew up in the pizza business. He worked with his family at his father's place, Tommy's. In 1978, Steve decided to strike out on his own to open his own pizzeria near the Ohio State University campus. Instead of calling it Steve's, he opted to use his last name on the sign. The pizzeria was set up in a former BFF restaurant at 1510 North High Street. (BFF stood for Burger Boy Food-O-Rama, though some said it meant Bigger, Better, Faster.) BFF was a chain of burger places popular in the Midwest in the 1960s. The location allowed Iacono to experiment with the drive-thru window in the building. Being a pizza business with plenty of parking and a patio near one of the largest concentrations of college students in the country made the business very popular. Iacono had survived a trial by fire by opening the restaurant during an OSU-Michigan home game.

In 1983, Iacono opened a second pizza restaurant on Kenny Road (in a former Leonardo's Pizza location). The Kenny Road location received a rave review from the restaurant writer at the *Columbus Dispatch*, Doral Chenoweth, in 1984, which helped grow business. Later in 1984, a location was opened on Sawmill Road, followed by locations in Dublin (Shawnee Hills) and Hilliard. Today, the Kenny Road and Dublin Road locations remain.

Steve's children, Trent, Monica and Emily, worked for the pizzerias while growing up, and Trent is still actively managing them today. Even though Steve "retired," he continued to be active in the business through 2020. Iacono's continues to do things the hard way. The dough, sausage, meatballs, noodles, some salad dressings and soups are still made in house throughout the week. Those who know of Steve's pizza heritage definitely see a difference between the pizza and other items served at Tommy's and those at Iacono's. There is a distinct difference, though both are great.

VILLA NOVA (1978)

Frank Colleli had a long association with pizza in Columbus. Among his operations were Frankie's Pizza in the 1960s on the Ohio State campus and Franco's Pizza, which he sold to Don Curly in 1976. (It closed in 2001.) Frank was known as an innovator and improviser in the local pizza business. He was very much a do-it-yourself owner, typically doing his own repairs on everything. In the early days of Frankie's, he was one of the first pizza businesses to offer delivery, and to improve efficiency, he put radios in the delivery cars. He was close friends with Richie DiPaolo, and the two loved to talk about pizza together. He was known to be a bit of a character, as well. One of his famous projects was an old Dodge pickup truck with a train honk mounted on it.

In 1978, Frank and his wife, Donna, converted the former Vogue Lounge from a bar to a bar and restaurant. The bar and kitchen take up one half of the building and the other half is guest seating. Villa Nova serves a wide variety of Italian fare, but with Frank's pizza heritage, it was a pizza destination for many. Frank and Donna retired to Florida in 1986. Their son John stayed on with the new owner and worked in the kitchen. John talked his father into buying the business back in 1998. Frank remained a fixture at Villa Nova until his death in 2014. At that time, sons Frankie and John, as well as John's wife, Meghan, took over the operation, and Donna retired again.

Frank and Donna's legacy is on display for guests whenever they enter the dining room or bar. Many years ago, Donna bought a few copper kettles on eBay and asked Frank if he could find a few more. The end result is over 350 kettles in the dining room. The prize of the collection is the world's smallest copper kettle, made out of a penny. It was featured on *Antiques Roadshow* in 2009.

Frank had an interest in copper gauges from the nineteenth and early twentieth centuries. Many of the gauges are still in working condition. Frank's fascination with gauges started early in life. His father was a locomotive engineer. Frank was in the Merchant Marines and was stationed in New Orleans. When he was not on a ship, he worked at an antique store on Bourbon Street, where he learned to restore old items. Today, there are over three hundred of the gauges at Villa Nova, and many are in the bar, along with an extensive license plate collection mounted on the walls. Frank worked hard to restore the kettles and gauges. Each took up to three days of work, using steel wool, acid, a sander and two to three coats of polyurethane.

Little has changed since Villa Nova opened in 1978, and the place is typically packed. Parking was often a challenge on the weekends, until the family bought the business next door (which was once a Just Pies location) and knocked it down to more than double the size of the parking lot. Villa Nova is known for having great daily specials to choose from seven days a week. The pizza remains a top seller and reflects the years of pizza experience Frank brought to the business.

Antolino's Pizza (1979)

Antolino's Pizza was started by Bob Snyder and his wife, Joy, in 1979. Before opening the business, he had invested countless hours perfecting his pizza sauce recipe. Bob came into the business with plenty of experience, as he had worked for Leonardo's Pizza for many years. Many of his longtime staff were Leonardo's alumni, as well. He knew enough about the business to know people might not rush out to buy "Snyder's Pizza." He asked his insurance agent, Ralph Antolino, if he could use his last name for the business. In addition to the authenticity connotated by an Italian surname, Synder ensured his *A* listing would be at the top of the choices in the pizza section of the yellow pages. The location had previously been known as Anna's Pizza and before that Bruno's.

Today, his son James continues his legacy at the shop after Bob had a stroke. The Morse Road pizzeria is especially known for its Monday night pizza special, which makes it the busiest night of the week for the business. This tradition dates to the early 1980s. James Snyder grew up in the business, and he was just a few years old when the pizzeria opened. "One of my first memories was reaching for a pop out of a multiple use cooler, and a cheese grinder head falling on my toe and breaking it," he recalled. As for his father, Bob, James shared, "My father, in starting the place, really only had one goal. That goal was for people to say, 'There goes Bob Snyder, and he makes a hell of a pizza.'" The Snyder family is still making a fine pizza today.

Kingy's Pizza Pub (1980)

If you head to Kingy's Pizza Pub, keep an eye out for Bert Reynolds. Not Burt Reynolds, Bert is the one who started Kingy's Pizza with his wife, Jonda, and brother, Rick. His father, Harley Reynolds, bought King Arthur's Steakhouse from a relative in 1980. The business struggled, and after about eighteen months, Harley turned the restaurant over to his sons. Neither had any restaurant experience. They decided that a steakhouse was too pricey for the area, but the perfect combination of pizza and beer was likely to be more successful. Rick, Bert and Jonda spent a few weeks with a lot of trial and error figuring out how to make the perfect pizza for their place. Kingy's Pizza was born.

It took a while for the business to click in Canal Winchester, which at the time, was a very small community, but the owners got a few breaks. In 1987, they entered the Eastside Pizza Challenge with their signature pizza, Kingy's All the Way—cheese, pepperoni, sausage, mushrooms, onions, green peppers, ham, hot peppers and anchovies, if you ask. One of the family members is always on-site, which helps maintain consistency in food and service. Many employees have been with the business for twenty or more years. Kingy's has faced some challenges. When the Ohio Department of Transportation started to widen SR 33, Kingy's needed to move. They were eventually able to secure some land about two hundred yards north of their location to build a new restaurant, but they had to put their houses on the line to finance the project.

The area has continued to have explosive growth, and Kingy's has grown with it. Kingy's has been noted as one of the highest earning single site pizzerias in the country. The family is also competitive. They have won pizza competitions at the local level, and two of their sandwiches received national

Bexley Pizza Plus award-winning pizza.

attention. The Reu-Bert sandwich is a longtime customer favorite. It is a two-pound Reuben sandwich piled with corned beef and pastrami and coated with homemade spicy Thousand Island dressing. It is named after Bert. It was one of almost two thousand entries in Restaurant Hospitality's 2014 Best Sandwiches competition, and it won top honors. Kingy's Italian Baller sandwich has also placed in the competition. Kingy's is a big operation but still has an atmosphere with a family feel. After years of hard work, Kingy's has become royalty in the restaurant business.

BEXLEY PIZZA PLUS (1982)

The origin of Bexley Pizza Plus began in 1980, when Don and Kathy Schmitt opened Pizza Man. In 1982, the old Toddle House building on East Broad Street became available in Bexley. (The Toddle House was a vibrant chain in the 1950s with over two hundred locations; many feel it was similar to Waffle House, no surprise since that company was started by a former Toddle House manager.) Before the Schmitts moved in, the previous tenant was Paul's Bagels. The new business was called Pizza Plus. Don and Kathy inherited an old rotating bagel oven with the space and put it to work making pizzas. Brad Rocco started working for Pizza Plus as a delivery driver in the same year while he was going to college. In 1984, a fire destroyed the oven and prompted a large renovation project for the building. Brad stayed on during the renovation, and when Pizza Plus reopened, he was a manager. This time, they had a new gas oven for pizzas. When the owners divorced, Brad bought out Kathy's share and was a co-owner by 1992. In 1996, indoor seating was added to the shop, ending a long span of pickup and carryout only sales.

In 1988, a second location was added, Gahanna Pizza Plus, in partnership with Jack Atlas, Rocco and Schmitt. (Today it is owned by Atlas and Schmitt.) In 2002, Brad was inspired to elevate his pizza prowess by the Columbus Pizza Challenge (Slice of Columbus today) when he won the First Place Judges Award. In 2003, the Gahanna Pizza Plus shop, including Brad Rocco and Jack Atlas, took their Ultimate Pizza (two types of mushrooms and two types of pepperoni) to what was then called the North American Pizza and Ice Cream Show (NAPICS) Pizza Pizzazz competition in Columbus. They won first place in the contest. The prize for winning the competition was an all-expense paid trip to Italy and an opportunity to compete in the World Pizza Championship as a member of the U.S. Pizza Team. Atlas and Rocco became members of the team to compete in the World Pizza Championship in Salsamaggiori, Italy, in 2003. The Food Network traveled with them and produced a show that featured the U.S. Pizza Team. That year, they received the second-highest scores out of all the Americans in the contest.

There were two more first place wins at NAPICS in 2005 and 2006. In 2010, Rocco scored fourth place in the Best Non-Traditional Pizza category at the International Pizza Challenge (IPC) in Las Vegas, followed by several regional wins at IPC. He kept his eye on the pizza pie prize and was awarded first place in the Best Traditional Pizza Category, which made him the world champion in 2014. The winning combination was Margherita and spicy pepperoni pizza with fresh and flash-blanched mushrooms. The very next year, 2015, Rocco won first place at the NAPICS Pizza Pizzazz. Those awards brought a lot of attention by the press, both locally and nationally. Pizza Plus had people coming to try its pizza from all over Ohio and even a few who drove from other states. While Rocco does like to win, what he enjoys the most about the competitions is the camaraderie in the pizza community and the opportunity to learn new techniques and share ideas with his peers. And a few trips to Italy does not hurt.

In 2006, CVS made an offer for the Bexley Pizza Plus building that could not be refused, including help to find a new location. There were limited spaces available that would keep Pizza Plus in Bexley, but eventually, a spot was found next door to Rubino's Pizza. Although this did not seem ideal to either business, the two have very different approaches to pizza, so there is not a concern about customer snatching. It is not uncommon for a car to park in either driveway and have the driver go into Pizza Plus while the passenger goes to Rubino's for pickups. The proximity of the two places helps those households that are divided on their pizza preferences stay together. The neighbors also help each other. Once, Pizza Plus lost access to hot water to make dough when its water heater died. Rubino's sent over enough water for Brad to make his dough for the day. Pizza Plus returned the favor to Rubino's when the mixer died.

The original Pizza Plus closed for one day to move the ovens and supplies to the new location. New multiple deck ovens were added to increase capacity. The new space also allowed the selection of toppings to grow to over forty choices. Pizza Plus has always been involved in supporting the

Bexley Pizza Plus crew in action, with Brad Rocco on right. *Courtesy of Columbus Underground and Pam Reece.*

Bexley community. It started selling pizzas for concessions at Bexley High School for football and other events. It typically sells fifty to seventy-five pizzas per night to football fans.

Brad has a long history in Bexley. He grew up in the house where famous Bexley writer and columnist Bob Greene lived. Greene wrote about Rubino's many times in his newspaper columns and in a book about his teenage years. Rocco also enjoyed Rubino's when he was growing up but was more diverse than Greene. He also spent time at Iacono's, Massey's, Little Sicily and Pizza House as a teenager. Brad remains involved in pizza events and the ongoing search for the perfect pizza combination. He is active in many pizza and cooking fan pages, events and competitions.

CATFISH BIFF'S (1983)

Catfish Biff's is a mainstay for late-night eating for south campus dormitories at Ohio State University. The old house predates the dorms that its pizza and subs are consumed in. The business has been under the eye of university property buyers looking to expand campus facilities for years. It was founded by Harold Hays and Steve Hucek in 1984, and the two had a lot of experience to bring to the operation. Hays was a restaurant management major at the Ohio State University. While attending OSU, he worked at a Cork N Cleaver restaurant. He eventually went to baking school to perfect his pizza crust. When Hays passed away in 2019, friends gathered at a well-known pizza place called DeArini's. Catfish Biff's is still on Eleventh Avenue, ready to feed college students and late-night revelers for carryout only, unless they can score a picnic table. The origin of the name has been lost to time, but the tagline is "we ain't got no fish."

DONATOS (1970–84)

Jim Grote ended the 1960s with a desire to grow his business, and his mission was to ensure consistency in product and service to meet his high standards. The 1970s would be his decade to put his plan into action. Many shops were still slicing pepperoni by hand. The result was a lot of labor, a lot of waste and inconsistent thickness of slices. Grote's solution was to create the Pepp-A-Matic, a manual machine to ensure each slice had the same thickness. He also started weighing ingredients so that each pizza would be the same. A spinoff of his efforts was the launch of the Grote Manufacturing Company in 1972. The company would go on to create solutions for frozen pizzas, pizza shops and all types of food businesses. Grote also started the shift to conveyor ovens at his pizzerias. Donatos was one of the first shops to use them, and the result was a consistent product. The original store on Thurman Avenue served as a testing ground for some of these innovations. Grote opened the second Donatos location on Brice Road in 1974. When Grote was sure both locations were meeting his goals, it was time to expand. Donatos had eight locations by 1984.

EZZO SAUSAGE COMPANY (1978)

Dominic Ezzo made sausage to sell at his Canastota, New York grocery store. His son John helped opened an Ezzo sausage plant in Indiana in the 1960s. John's son Bill Ezzo was recruited to play as a wide receiver at Ohio State University for Woody Hayes. This brought him to Columbus. When the Indiana factory was destroyed by an electrical fire, John's oldest son,

Box of Sausage for Pizza (SFP) from DiPaolo Foods (probably from 1960s).

Scott, was sent forth to scout out a new home for Ezzo Sausage. A location was found on the south side of Columbus, and it was time for the grinding to begin. Bill was recruited to sell sausage and soon found that there was a huge demand for pepperoni, so the Ezzos set about perfecting their own pepperoni recipe. The main supplier of pepperoni for Columbus experienced a strike at its factory and then had supply issues, and Ezzo had the right product at the right time. The Ezzos worked with local pizzeria owners to make sure their product met the needs for flavor and thickness. An early customer was Domino's, but the chain grew too fast for Ezzo to keep up with demand.

In 2016, Ezzo relocated to the west side of Columbus and built a state-of-the-art factory, which was mammoth compared to its old Lockbourne Road location. Bill's sons, Darren and Jonathan, grew up working in the factory, folding boxes and doing other tasks under the watchful eye of their dad. When Bill "retired" to Florida, he continued to sometimes monitor the factory by video camera. Today, Ezzo is considered one of the finest artisan pepperonis in the world and is highly sought after, even in the very parochial pizzerias of New York City.

Pepperoni and SFP

Pepperoni is an American invention, though the name does have an Italian origin. *Peperoni* is the plural of *peperone*, the Italian word for bell pepper. American pepperoni was probably inspired by the spicy dry sausages that were popular in Naples and the salami of Southern Italy. Pepperoni is typically softer and usually a blend of pork and beef seasoned with paprika or another chili pepper to give it a red hue. It was probably created in the early 1900s in New York City. Today, there are two main styles of pepperoni, American and traditional. American pepperoni does not cup and char like traditional pepperoni.

Before pepperoni as we know it, meat plants made SFP, Sausage for Pizza. It was a smoked paprika spicy sausage, cooked, chilled and then sliced. This saved time and money because it did not require the drying and aging process of traditional pepperoni. As a result, it became very popular with pizzerias. In the 1980s, pizzerias started to look for the more old-school style of pepperoni, which created a niche that the Ezzo Sausage Company has continued to fill. Its pepperoni is special because it is 100 percent beef and pork—no fillers or other additives. Ezzo also perfected a way to dry its

THE NAME GAME

Early pizza menus and ads in Columbus seem to have a difficult time deciding if a place that sold pizza was a *pizzeria* or *pizzaria*. As time progressed to the 1960s, we see a firm shift to the term *pizzeria*, with many businesses trading out an *a* for an *e*. The first time the term appeared in the *Merriam-Webster Dictionary* was 1912. By the 1930s, it started to be commonly used. Some believe the spelling might have been influenced by the rapid expansion of cafeterias in the same era. Others suggest that the word comes from the Italian word for pie/pizza and the suffix of -era, which indicates "a place for."

A name is important to a business. In the case of a pizzeria, an Italian-sounding name adds a certain credibility to the pie served. Don Potts and Jim Grote saw the value of using Donatos instead of their own surnames. Ruben Cohen went with Rubino's. Bob Snyder borrowed his insurance agent's last name, Antolino, for an authentic Italian name and, more importantly, to make sure he was listed at the top of the Yellow Pages pizza listing. Rich Floyd chose to call the pizzeria he won in a card game Cardo's.

Over time, there was confusion—sometimes bordering on pandemonium—related to pizzeria names. People showed up to Ricardi's in Beechwold instead of Ricardo's on Oakland Park. Chef Casino had one location on Cleveland Avenue. Casino Pizza had three locations, with one on Cleveland Avenue. Which John is making your pizza? Johnny's Pizza, Johnny's Pizza and Subs or Johnny Remali's Pizza. The Romeo's Pizza of today has no connection to the Romeo's that Columbus discovered in 1950, the trademark on the name of Sirij and Massey's place lapsed over time.

pepperoni without a casing, which makes it easier to slice. Pepperoni was typically an appetizer in the early twentieth century but started to appear on pizzeria menus in 1950, which placed Columbus on the cutting edge for growing the pepperoni trend. Today, pepperoni is the most common topping and is found on about 50 percent of pizzas nationwide. In Columbus, we are likely a bit over that mark.

PIZZA PEAKS (1985–99)

he late 1980s and 1990s was the era of Columbus as a preeminent city for pizza lovers. It was named by *Pizza Today Magazine* as the Pizza Capital of the USA in 1994. The number for pizza parlors per capita peaked, with over 450 pizzerias tossing dough all over town. Donatos was on the rise and growing locations. Massey's was primed for growth, and local independents were still holding their own over national chains—in contrast to most other communities across the country. Cassano's Pizza in Dayton had started expanding into Columbus in the 1970s but was starting to falter and closed the last Columbus location by the time leg warmers went out of style.

PLANK'S CAFE AND PIZZERIA (1985)

Plank's Cafe at 742 Parsons Avenue has a long history. In 1939, Walter Plank bought Mann's Cafe after being a longtime customer. The Manns bought the building in 1919, and before them, the space had been a saloon since 1886.

Walter Plank Jr. started helping his dad when he returned from World War II. By the time his father passed away in 1961, he was managing the family business, which was serving three meals a day six days per week. Walter Plank Jr. continued expanding the menu and the square footage, building

Signature pizza from Plank's Bier Garten. *Courtesy of Katie Trigg and Plank's Bier Garten.*

an addition that doubled the space. In 1985, he decided to add a pizza oven, which is when Plank's became a destination for pizza. Plank's Pizza quickly became a favorite of German Village diners and people outside the neighborhood. One secret to the success of the pizza is the extra sugar added to the dough. Even though there are other Plank's locations, regulars are very tribal in their loyalty to pizza at the Parsons location. Walter Plank Jr. was a 1941 graduate of Saint Charles High School and maintained a relationship with his alma mater for the rest of his lifetime. Walt Plank Field at the high school is named in his honor.

In 1960, Willy Plank, one of Walt's sons, ventured south to open Plank's Bier Garten on South High Street. The Bier Garten started serving pizza in 1996 (determined by looking at the manufacture date of its original oven). The pizza at the Bier Garten is different than the Parsons location. According to general manager John McGinnis, the dough has minimal sugar and uses whole eggs. Dan Plank was a baker at Thurn's, and in addition to his own baking experience, he conversed with staff at Donatos for additional advice on ingredient ratios and other specifics. The perception that the pizza at the different locations is different is exactly right.

Adriatico's (1985)

Adriatico's has been a mainstay on the Ohio State University campus since opening in 1987. Pizza is always popular on any college campus, but Adriatico's stood out with consistently good service, reasonable prices and a high-quality product. Dough is made daily for the thick Sicilian, true-to-form New York style (regular) and extra thin pizza. Owner Greg Fortney had a good business, and the pizza was frequently mentioned in the college paper, the *Lantern*, as the best pizza on campus.

In the fall of 2017, Ohio State University announced a plan to take the Adriatico's building as part of an expansion for the OSU Optometry program, but a firm date was not certain. Some state of panic developed as rumors started to circulate, but Fortney made it clear that Adriatico's would continue on campus. Adriatico's fans spent half of 2018 in a state of limbo. No new site could ever reflect the character of the original Adriatico's, which calls a small, century-old brick building home. The university and Adriatico's were committed to finding a spot near the original location. For Adriatico's, this would be an opportunity for a larger kitchen and more dining space. For many, but especially south campus dorm students and all of the nursing staff of the OSU Medical Center, Adriatico's was more than just food; it was a public service and, in many cases, a critical need. The Monday and Tuesday Buckeye Pizza Special—an eighteen-by-twenty-four sheet of Sicilian-style pizza that can feed at least ten people with ease is offered at a value price. Cheap pizza is rarely outstanding, but this a great pizza at a great price.

In the early spring of 2018, word came out of a new location for Adriatico's. It will be just around the corner at 1681 Neil Avenue. The new location is an upgrade in many ways: more dining space, more craft beer selection and a larger kitchen, which equals a greater choice of items on the menu. Parking was a challenge before and is not easy at the new location; however, most conveniently, guests with pickup orders can park in the loading zone directly in front of the entrance, which makes access to Adriatico's so much easier. Adriatico's has more than survived the transition to the new location; it is thriving more than ever without losing any of the qualities that made it a great pizza parlor. The transition from the old spot to the new address only resulted in one day of down time. The new Adriatico's is just a few hundred feet from the original spot. Salvaged from internment in a landfill, the original front door is mounted in a place of honor between the bathrooms in the new location.

Left: Interior of the original Adriatico's Pizza on Eleventh Avenue shortly before moving.

Below: New York–style pizza with extra sauce at Adriatico's Pizza. (The wedding pizza for the author.)

(The Other) Adriatico's—Cincinnati (1974)

There is another Adriatico's. It opened in 1974 in Cincinnati. It moved several times in the Clifton area before landing at an expanded location in 2011. Tom Erbeck purchased the business in 1999. The menus are similar to our beloved Columbus location, but its Buckeye is called the Bearcat in honor of the University of Cincinnati mascot.

ENRICO'S (1988)

Regular or even infrequent visitors at Enrico's are often on a first-name basis with Tiziana, who runs the front of house of this small, modest restaurant tucked in a strip development on the border of Dublin. She and her family commuted a long way to start their business—they are all first-generation Italian immigrants to central Ohio. They settled in Grandview in 1968. Tiziana's mother, Angelina, worked as a seamstress, and Ottavio, her father, found work in construction. Both parents liked to cook, so when Tiziana's uncle opened Dante's Pizza in Clintonville in 1973, it was only natural that they would lend a hand. Her mother's brother Joe Apollino had arrived several years earlier and learned the pizza business while working a variety of positions at Leonardo's, an iconic Columbus pizzeria chain.

All of the family members worked at Dante's at different times over the years. The family, now including Tiziana's husband, Rick, decided to open Enrico's in March 1988. (Guess where Rick met his wife—while working at Dante's.) The restaurant started as a scratch kitchen and has remained that way since day one. They make their own dough, sauce, pastas (especially the beloved raviolis), house salad dressing, meatballs and sausage. One thing the restaurant does that few shops still practice is grinding cheese from blocks of provolone instead of using pre-shredded cheese. The owners have not changed a menu item since opening in 1988, and if they did, "our customers would tell us." It has always been a word-of-mouth business; they do not advertise and don't offer coupons. Enrico's has a loyal base of regular customers who plan in advance for the two times per year that the business closes for a week for vacation (Easter and Fourth of July). Tiziana says one of the best aspects of running the business is watching families grow up with Enrico's and seeing customers bring their children and then seeing the next generation of children grow up and bring in their own children. Special orders are not uncommon, with some customers asking for their pizza extra crispy, triangle cut or with all the pepperoni on top. Longtime customers are familiar with seeing Tiziana by the front counter greeting customers while "mom and pop" are in the back in their kitchen whites cooking away.

Where does the name Enrico come from? The restaurant is named for one of Tiziana's cousins from Abruzzo. They have visited each other in their respective home cities many times over the years. Maybe one day one of Enrico's children will continue the tradition of coming to Columbus, starting a pizza place and naming it in honor of a relative.

PASQUALE'S PIZZA AND PASTA (1988)

The original Pasquale's Pizza and Pasta opened in 1988 in Uptown Westerville. The building that housed it had been a culinary landmark in Westerville since the turn of the twentieth century; it was home to Williams Grill and the Crystal Room through the 1960s. Jim Francisco brought a lot of passion to the project, but he had a secret weapon—one of this team had worked for a well-known pizzeria. In 2015, Francisco sold the business to Megan Ada, who would open Asterisk Supper Club in the space on North State Street. The new Pasquale's Pizza and Pasta House opened on Schrock Road by the end of 2015 to replace the original. Francisco's son and daughter-in-law, Anthony and Catherine Francisco, opened Pasquale's Pizza and Pub on Ryan Parkway in 2015. Having doubled their pizza possibilities, the residents of Westerville have moved on from losing the original spot. Both locations are much easier to access for pickup.

GRANDAD'S PIZZA (1989)

Grandad's pizza is a family affair. Granddad's is not related to Grandma's Pizza, nor is it connected to Cousin Vinny's Pizza. Stephen Baumann opened Grandpa's Pizza on Morse Road in 1989. He is related to the family behind Donatos Pizza. Grandad's is definitely not like Donatos. The Grandad's Pizza locations in Grandview (1997) and Hilliard (2015) are owned by his cousin. Stephen is also the co-owner of Katie's Pizza in Gahanna. The original Grandad's on Morse Road is a barebones carryout operation known for

94

being generous with toppings and value priced, even with delivery. Provolone is smoked in house and makes a great addition on the Cheese Lovers Deluxe Pizza with mozzarella, smoked provolone, cheddar jack, parmesan, romano and feta. All of the Grandad's Pizza locations share one thing in common: the signature green shamrock on the pizza box.

Figlio (1991)

Peter Danis met Laurie when they were in law school at the Ohio State University. After graduation, they embarked on legal careers and started a life together. Just before their first daughter was born, the two decided to leave their legal careers to pursue something they could be as passionate about as the joy of their first child. The two spent countless hours in their kitchen perfecting the recipes for pizzas and pastas that they would feature at the restaurant they opened in 1991, Figlio Wood Fired Pizza. Their neighbor was Domino's Pizza. The Grandview location quickly took off with many favorable reviews. Among Figlio's greatest fans was the Grumpy Gourmet, Doral Chenoweth. Figlio landed in his top-ten restaurants list for many years, and that trend has continued to this day. Figlio remains among the most highly ranked restaurants in Columbus. The restaurant is also notable for frequent appearances in the Where I Eat feature in the *Columbus Dispatch*. Other accolades include a mention as one of the top one hundred independent pizzerias in *Pizza Today* magazine in 2006. One of its recipes appears in *The Italian American Cookbook: A Feast of Food from a Great American Cooking* by John and Galina Mariani.

Figlio began with a focus on wood fired pizzas and house-made pastas. The Danises make their own dough and are passionate about ingredients. Many dishes have been inspired by their travels. Figlio has continued to be progressive in more than just recipes and a wood fired oven. The restaurant has been a pathfinder in buying local ingredients, recycling food waste and even buying energy credits to offset the utility use of the business. Figlio was a nonsmoking establishment long before the city instituted a smoking ban for restaurants and public spaces. Peter served as president of the central Ohio Restaurant Association in 2000. The Upper Arlington and Grandview locations hosted a Take Your Tomato to Figlio week, allowing customers to bring in their own tomatoes. Figlio donated one dollar to the Mid-Ohio Foodbank for each caprese salad made with a customer's tomato.

The passion the couple has for recipe development and perfection once led to a revolt by their children. Laura served a chicken picatta dish at home every night for six weeks, and the kids finally had enough chicken. Guests can order a standard pepperoni pizza at Figlio or they can create their own from a long list of ingredients. Examples of more nontraditional pies from Figlio's constantly evolving menu include pear and brie (with blue cheese, prosciutto and arugula) and pesto chicken with feta (with chicken, roasted red peppers, kalamatas, tomatoes, pine nuts, feta and basil pesto sauce).

Peter and Laurie added a Figlio in Upper Arlington and another in Dayton. They also included their passion for wine by adding Vino Vino adjacent to Figlio in 2004. In addition to fantastic wine pairings and flights, the restaurant also offers fare that is different than Figlio. Menus were designed by their eldest daughter, Kelvin. The couple began their interest in wine when they traveled to Florida together for spring break during law school.

In addition to adding restaurants, the Danis family grew, too, with a total of three daughters. While staying busy with the business, the family maintained a tradition of having a family meal, even if it was late at night after closing the restaurant.

HOUNDDOGS 3 DEGREE PIZZA/PIZZA FOR THE PEOPLE (1993)

Jeff Stewart opened Hounddogs Pizza in 1993. At the time, he did have a hound dog, but he had to give the dog to a friend because he was spending so much time at the restaurant. Originally, the business was called Hounddog's Three Degree Pizza. This was because it offered three types of sauce: traditional/regular, spicy and Howlin' Hot Sauce. Today, Hounddogs offers five types of sauce (pesto and Smokin Joe's sauce were added) and three types of crust (traditional, Smokin' Joes and gluten free). Smokin' Joe's–style pizzas account for over one half of the sales at the business. The style involves a thick crust ring infused with garlic and a slightly spicy red sauce, and the pizza is cut in triangles instead of squares.

When Hounddogs opened, it was mainly a carryout and delivery business and was open twenty-four hours a day, seven days a week. When dining space was added later, the combination of pizza at any hour and the Old North Columbus location's proximity to campus, eclectic Clintonville and the SoHud community made it a magnet for artists, musicians and a diverse

Breakfast pizza at Hounddog's.

range of clientele. The tagline changed from Three Degree Pizza to Pizza for the People. Several years later, when Hounddogs' neighbor West Coast Video closed, Stewart took over the space and transformed it into the Ravari Room. This space was a combination bar and music venue, drawing local, regional and national acts, featuring punk, metal, jazz and more. The Ravari Room is no longer a music venue, other than karaoke. Several concert posters created by local artists are framed on the back wall to give a hint of the bands that the space used to host.

In January 2015, Hounddogs shifted to different hours. It is no longer an all-day, all-night operation, though the hours are still very accessible— open 9:00 a.m. to 2:30 a.m. each day of the week. The menu features several memorable specialty pizzas. Staying true to its early-morning roots, the breakfast pizza has a base of spicy queso, cheddar, ham, spicy sausage, bacon, red onions and green peppers and is topped with fresh scrambled eggs and French fries. It is served with a side of maple syrup. The Hot Mama offers hot Cajun links cut into small pieces, ham, bacon and sauerkraut with a spicy sauce. A memorable side is the house-made lasagna bites served with a side of marinara. The pieces of lasagna are breaded and deep fried.

The decor of Hounddogs leaves a lasting impression. Thick wooden booths line both sides of the dining area and bar. Much of the interior work was created by Stewart. The large wooden back door looks like it was salvaged from an ancient castle, but in reality, it was created with leftover scrap wood from the construction of the bar area. The hood of a former delivery vehicle is mounted on the wall. There is a classic beer can collection, plus a host of other items crafted by Stewart. The dining area wall features a large mural of various characters one might see in a late-night eatery, created by an artist known as Brett Superstar.

Hounddogs has had a host of memorable delivery vehicles. The original debuted in 1997. This delivering dog star was born as nontraditional marketing. The inspiration came late one night. Owner Jeff Stewart had a vision of a hound dog strapped to a rocket that he could mount to a classic car he had recently acquired. Stewart started the project the next morning. The original dog was made by a local artist, Mike Foley. Stewart called Columbus College of Art and Design to find a sculptor and was eventually referred to a former student. When asked about his credentials, Foley replied, "Come

Hounddog's delivery mobile

Hound dog on side of Hounddog's delivery mobile.

over to my house on Indianola to see my work." Stewart found a house filled with sculptures of all sizes and shapes and knew he had found the right person to craft his canine.

The first night out was quite memorable. The rocket was sheared off the dog when it caught on a low-hanging parking garage roof. Since then, things have really taken off for the car and the pizza joint. There have been three rockets over the years. The second was remounted on the original hound dog and then attached (in order) to a 1971 Cadillac Coupe de Ville (1997–2001), a 1988 VW Golf (2002–3) and a 1985 Cadillac Fleetwood Broughham Limo (2003–13). After a hiatus, a new dog with a new rocket was mounted on a red 1962 Cadillac Fleetwood in the summer of 2015. The new car is like the original, with a diamondback plate mounted on the roof as a base for a hallowed hound dog, creating an unforgettable delivery vehicle.

Lost Planet Pizza and Pasta (1996–98)

To describe Ricky Barnes as eclectic would be an understatement at best. He is not an out-of-the-box thinker because he would not be boxed in and would somehow make it a circle. Ricky is a folk artist who dabbles in painting and sculpture. He is a musician who plays several instruments and sings in bands, including the Savory Chickens and the Hoot Owls. He was once the co-owner of a skateboard shop. What he is most noted for, though, is cooking. He was a celebrated chef at Rigsby's and Lindeys. One of his soups received rave reviews from Doral Chenoweth, the Grumpy Gourmet. In May 1993, he opened the Galaxy Cafe in Powell with Jerry Burgos. The menu would be considered progressive and eclectic, even by today's standards, with Cuban, southwestern and multiple other influences. A Galaxy Cafe in Grandview followed.

In 1996, inspired by a thin, flatbread-style pizza he had at a place in Chicago, he opened Lost Planet Pizza and Pasta in the Short North. The flavor combination blended traditional ingredients with a twist and plenty of nontraditional topping. The menu constantly changed, typically offering ten to twelve pizza varieties and ten to twelve pastas, as well some very non-Italian appetizers, like black bean hummus and garlic roasted potato pancakes. An example of a typical nontypical pizza at Lost Planet is the Roast Chicken Pizza, with cracker-thin crust, roasted chicken, tomato basil chutney, cumin mozzarella and roasted corn. Another example is Blackened Chicken Caesar Pizza, again with cracker-thin crust and blackened chicken, romaine lettuce, Caesar dressing and parmesan cheese. At one point, the restaurant offered a lunchtime buffet with multiple pizzas and pastas and a few other items. Some diners viewed this as an incredible deal that bordered on a public service. Regular customers did not talk about this to others to reduce the competition in line. In 2001, Ricky's Galaxy exploded. He had divested himself of the other restaurants earlier and abruptly shuttered his last restaurant to be a resort chef in Taos, New Mexico, for a few years.

Benny's Pizza Marysville (1996)

Fred and Robin Neumeier purchased Benny's Pizza in January 1996. Neumeier had good training for the business he would build at Benny's, as he had the Bogey Inn for many years. The original building was Frost Top

Root Beer Stand and was complete with carhops. The stand opened in 1958, featuring a revolving Root Beer Mug on the roof. The mug is still there today, but it stopped turning long ago. The owners also decided to preserve the legacy of the space by brewing root beer on site. They added a bar with a large selection of beer. A relationship began with Elevator Brewing, which was in Marysville at the time and continued after Elevator moved to Columbus. For many years, it brewed a special beer just for Benny's. With great pizza, a wide selection of beverages, other food choices and free popcorn, Benny's quickly became a popular hangout for locals. The Neumeier's expanded the original space and added an outdoor patio, giving guests over ten thousand square feet. The patio featured bands several days a week. Neumeier and manager Neal Hemmert collected a large number of nostalgic sports items with a largely Ohio focus to fill the bar space and beyond. There is also a selection of rock and country music souvenirs, with a multitude of signed photographs and other items, including one of Eric Clapton's guitars

The pizza is served on elevated pizza trays, and a wide variety of selections are offered. Longtime favorites include the Five Meat Pizza, with spicy smoked sausage, pepperoni, meatballs, Capicola ham and Italian sausage, as well as the Garbage, with pepperoni, Italian sausage, spicy smoked sausage, onions, mushrooms, green peppers, ham, tomatoes, black olives, green olives, bacon, pineapple, hot peppers and jalapeño peppers. Anchovies will be added if requested. Dough is still made fresh every day. Today, the space has three bars, so there is a need for a lot of pizza to feed hungry people between sips.

MASSEY'S 4.0 (1985–99)

Phillip Casa opened a commissary at the company's headquarters in Blacklick in 1988, with an eye on expansion. The commissary had the capacity to service the needs of at least twenty locations. By 1999, there were six company-owned Massey's Pizzas and one owned by former employee Randy Hicks. Cash flow trickled away, and by early October 1999, Casa was out of dough. The six company locations were closed without notice as Casa prepared to file for bankruptcy. Offers from Donatos and Hicks had been turned down prior to the closure. At the eleventh hour, two of Casa's cousins came calling.

Dave and Jed Pallone had a lot of business experience between them, and over the years, they developed a knack for knowing what people wanted and then creating it for them. They were owners of several popular clubs in Columbus, including Club Dance, Rosie O'Grady's, King Tut and Screaming Willy's. The brothers had funds from selling their TV station, Channel 62, the previous year. Both had a long-standing appetite for the pizza business. Jed worked at Leonardo's from 1961 to 1965, and Dave started delivering for Leonardo's in 1957. Dave went into the army, and when he came back, in 1968, he teamed up with Jed to start the Cabaret on the OSU campus, on Twelfth Avenue. Pizza was the main draw here. The brothers bought Massey's in October 1999 and had all six locations reopened by the beginning of 2000.

DONATOS (1985–99)

In 1987, Donatos had doubled the number of locations to fifteen in central Ohio. Television ads also launched in the same year. In 1991, the first Donatos outside of Columbus opened in Zanesville. It was operated by a former Donatos employee and was the first franchise of the company. In 1992, Donatos opened a new office in Gahanna and started to expand franchise opportunities throughout Ohio. By 1993, Donatos had grown to fifty locations, making it one of the largest pizza companies in the United States. The growth of Donatos caught the attention of the makers of the Big Mac. McDonald's looked at about sixty different pizza companies around the United States and, in 1999, found that Donatos was the company it wanted to diversify its market share. McDonald's made an offer, and Donatos accepted. When Donatos became part of the McDonald's empire, some called the new entity McDonatos.

SLICE OF COLUMBUS/COLUMBUS PIZZA CHALLENGE

What we know as the Slice of Columbus started as the Columbus Pizza Challenge in 1990. From the start, the event was about two things: large-scale consumption of a variety of pizza and support for a local charity, Nationwide Children's Hospital. The event changed names in 2007 to Slice of Columbus. Guests are able to enjoy slices of pizza from twenty or more pizzerias from Columbus. They also get to vote on their favorite pizza.

Slice of Columbus. *Courtesy of @CraveColumbus/Kayla Ketterer.*

Judges also sample each of the contestants for judges' awards. The event has grown over the years from a few hundred attendees to over one thousand. It is a lot of work for the pizzerias. Some bring ovens they can use on site, while others work out relays of delivery teams to keep them stockpiled with boxes of pizza through the night. Winning either the people's choice award or one of the judges' awards is a mark of pride for the pizzerias, so they make sure they offer the best they can plate for the table. The event is good exposure for new pizza businesses, and an award can tempt new customers to try out a place they had not heard of before. Several pizzerias listed in this book have won numerous awards at Slice of Columbus over the years.

ITALIAN FESTIVAL—ST. JOHN'S PIZZA (1999)

When the Italian Festival started in Columbus in 1980, it was at the Ohio State Fairgrounds. The festival had a focus on food, so of course, pizza was a requirement. Vince Millitello teamed up with several members of the Carfanga family and Bill Mansour to supply pizza for the masses. The Millitellos and the Carfangas have a long history of supplying Italian ingredients throughout Columbus. The families are cousins. The Millitellos came to Columbus in 1937 to open the Militello Macaroni Company. Saturnino (Sam) Carfagna opened a store selling Italian meats and groceries on Cleveland Avenue in 1937. Over time, the Millitellos focused on wholesale, and the Carfangas focused on retail. Both families knew pizza well. Vince's father gave Tommy Iacono his first order of supplies to start his pizza place in 1952.

When the festival started in 1980, there was no way to know what to expect for attendance. At the end of Saturday (the first day), the pizza supply was wiped out, so Vince and the team spent most of the night and morning prepping ingredients for Sunday. Pizza was clearly a hit and would remain a tradition for the festival.

In 1999, the festival was moved to St. John's Catholic Church in Italian Village, where pizza was made on site. For the first few years, Billy Colasante of Pizza House and Kevin Pica of Geno's ran the pizza operation. In 2001, Vince Millitello had moved back to Columbus after a long time away for work. His uncle Adam Carfanga, who was the chairman of the food committee,

Pizza served at St. John the Baptist Church during the Columbus Italian Festival. *Courtesy Jodi Miller Photography.*

asked Vince to be his co-chair. There might have been an alternative motive on the part of Carfanga because he retired from the chair position after the festival was over.

Millitello wanted to add a second pizza choice to the lineup, so in addition to the traditional round pizzas, the festival would feature thicker, square Sicilian pizza. Over the years, Millitello, who continues to work in food distribution, tweaked the recipe for the pizzas. The dough is now made to his specifications by the Venezia Bread Company. At least 1,250 pizza crusts are prepared, which means that well over ten thousand people are served during the course of the festival. The crust has a light and airy texture with a lot of flavor. Each pizza is hand cut. Twenty cases of pepperoni and forty cases of cheese (half mozzarella and half provolone) are used. A different type of pepperoni (old-school cup and char) is used for the Sicilian pizza. Each pan is dressed with oil before baking. Because of these special arrangements, the only time people can have this exact recipe is at the Italian Festival.

Some traditions have continued over the years. The Saturday before the festival, the pizza team gets together at the Carfangas' production facility to make two hundred gallons of pizza sauce. They have some coffee and donuts, and perhaps wine, while they do all of the work. After the work is done, they will head down the street for pizza and beer. The night before the

MILITELLO MEMORIES

The Millitello family has a long history of working with the food community in central Ohio. The following are a few memories Vince Millitello has of growing up in the industry.

Tommy Iacono was a photographer before he started in the pizza business. He was friends with Vince Millitello Sr. and his father, Gaspar.

Romeo Sirij of Romeo's Pizza appears in many of the older Millitello family photos, and he did work for the company at one time.

While working for his family business in the late 1960s, Millitello recalls taking the Watterson High School football team with him to the rail depot, where they were paid twenty dollars each and were given lunch to unload train cars full of tomatoes. It was a daylong job.

festival, all of the recipes are tested and shared among the volunteers. A few pizzas are typically sent to WBNS 10TV to help promote the festival. Sports anchor Dom Tiberi is a huge supporter of the event.

Proceeds from the sales go to the church, so St. John's does a lot to support the pizza team between festivals. The ovens and some other supplies are stored in the church garage. The pizza started in deck ovens before the group bought Carfanga's old ovens. Today, to keep up with growing demand, they use conveyor ovens. As a possible act of God, the storage facility for the older ovens caught fire, which destroyed the ovens and other equipment. The insurance payment gave them the budget to get the more efficient ovens. Semi-trailers are also used to store some of the equipment and are parked off-site until needed the next year.

The festival is definitely a team effort among the Italian food community. RDP brings a refrigerated trailer for vendors to store their food. Carfanga's donates all of the sauce, meatballs and pasta for the spaghetti dinners. Countless people have donated their time for decades. As Italian Village has grown and changed, volunteers have been harder to recruit, and with the uncertainty around COVID-19, the future of the festival is in question. It was canceled for the fall of 2020.

PIZZA SAVER (1985)

The 1980s was an age of exploration for pizza technology. One of the simplest but most helpful inventions was what is often called the Pizza Saver or the Pizza Tent. It was invented with the name of package saver by Carmela Vitale of Long Island. She submitted the patent in 1983, and it was approved in 1985 and put to use quickly. Her goal was to protect pizzas, cakes and pies from being squashed. Made from plastic, this three-legged table is placed in the center of the pizza to protect the pizza from being crushed by the lid of the box. Some have been critical of the waste this single-use item creates. In response, some pizza shops have tried other options, including placing a ball of uncooked dough in the center of the pizza as a sustainable alternative. Whether you are pro or con on the Pizza Saver debate, one unexpected aspect of the design is how people repurpose them. They have been used for tables in doll houses, egg holders, platforms for phones and more.

PIZZA TECH

Pizza is the most competitive segment in the restaurant business. Anything that saves time or money or that can improve quality will be relentlessly chased by a chain or a single shop. A few pennies saved per pizza can make a huge difference when competing in the pizza wars. The technology of pizza has been evolving for over one hundred years. As a competitive marketplace, the pizza industry has often been at the cutting edge of new food service innovations. For example, the first online order for food was in 1994 at Pizza Hut.

THERMAL INSULATED PIZZA BAG (1986)

Many different approaches have been used to keep a pizza warm during delivery. Primitive delivery bags to retain heat and heated boxes were in use in the early 1960s but were only mildly helpful. Ingrid Kosar of Wisconsin submitted her patent request in 1984, and it was approved in 1986. Her goal was similar to Vitale's, to protect the pizza. Her future business partner challenged her to create a thermal bag that could meet the Domino's standard for pizza heat retention: 140 degrees for forty-five minutes. She met that mark and Thermal Bags by Ingrid was born. Her first large sales order was with Domino's Pizza.

7

PIZZA PERMUTATIONS (2000-20)

fter surviving the non-crisis of Y2K, the palate of Columbus was clearly expanding and diversifying as the city began a new century. As the city continued to grow and draw in more transplants from around the country and all over the world, the concept of pizza and expectations for it started to change. It was not just native New Yorkers getting incensed by the square-cut cracker pizzas that permeated the city, but college kids and avid foodies also started to look and ask for different types of pizza. The new century marked a slowdown in the typical mom-and-pop pizza shop, as artisan pizza started to be less of a novelty and more of a norm.

Mama Mimi's (2000)

Jeff Aufdencamp met his future wife, Jodi, when they both worked at One Nation restaurant (at the top of the Nationwide building from 1977 to 1997). Jeff was from Toledo, and Jodie hailed from Iowa. Together they worked for the who's who of Columbus restaurants of the era: Chef Hartmut Handke, the Doody family (Sue at Lindey's and her sons, Chris and Rick, at Bravo) and Kyle Katz, who owned Barcelona and Magnolia. The two were with Bravo when they were asked to be part of the team tasked with opening a new location in Indianapolis and then Dayton.

Worn out by long hours and too much time away from their young children and each other, they headed back to Columbus. Jeff started to get interested in pizza and made them at work after the bar closed at Bravo. He became such a proponent for pizza that he suggested Kyle Katz add a pizza at Barcelona. Jeff and Jodi saw an article about take-and-bake in a trade magazine, which sparked an idea of trying to do it themselves. Then they tried a take-and-bake pizza while visiting Jodi's mother in Iowa, and the two were hooked.

In February 2000, the first location of Mama Mimi's Take and Bake opened on Henderson Road in a former catering kitchen of the 55 Group. In the beginning, it was just Jeff and Jodie and one full-time employee with a colorful history. The business allowed them to spend time together and bring the kids in when they wanted to.

The first big break for the business was winning a pizza contest at the Midwest Pizza Pizzazz competition in 2001. Shortly after, Jon Christensen, a restaurant writer for the *Dispatch*, wrote a review of their place. Sales tripled shortly thereafter, and they had a hard time keeping up with demand.

In 2002, Roger Gentile, owner of Gentile's the Wine Sellers in Grandview, asked them to take over a space that was formerly a small deli in the wine shop. It was a perfect fit for both; customers could grab a bottle of wine and pizza for the evening. Jeff and Jodi knew Roger from the restaurant business, as Roger was one of the foremost wine experts in town.

Then the Aufdencamps started to franchise, and the first location was in Dayton in 2005. At the peak of business, there were eight Mama Mimi's in Columbus, Dayton and Iowa. During this time, other take-and-bake companies, including the very successful Papa Murphy's, came to Columbus, but none could get a foothold. Jeff credits a focus on quality and customer service on surviving and thriving during the fierce competition from large chains.

The year 2006 was a benchmark for Mama Mimi's. It was presented with the Pizza of the Year award, given at the world's largest pizza trade show in Las Vegas. It won by cooking pizza in a regular home oven found at the show. To beat the other competitors using professional top-of-the-line ovens was a real accomplishment. The winning pizza was Mama's Marmalletta Amore, with chicken, caramelized onions, shredded mozzarella and provolone, gorgonzola cheese, fresh basil and hot pepper flakes.

The goal of the couple when they started and continued was to make sure their pizza was better than what people could have delivered.

On Christmas Eve 2009, Jodi was diagnosed with cancer. After a long battle with the disease, including a remission, she died in August 2012. Jeff credits many people with his ability to keep himself and the business going after Jodi's death. Rick and Chris Doody from Bravo gave him lessons on how to manage money and other operational tasks that Jodi had covered, as well as a lot of moral support, especially when his wife was sick. The Doodys often brought over food. Cameron Mitchell was a big help too. Jeff faced a number of challenges and pitfalls with the business while Jodi was ill and after she passed away, but he persevered to keep all three Columbus locations open and growing.

Today, he has had to contend with the trend of delivery and figuring out ways to match up with the right delivery service. Incorporating a pickup or delivery option in the Mama Mimi's website helped increase sales. A lost delivery customer is a lost sale, so Jeff embraces it. During the beginning of the COVID-19 era, his sales jumped up to a point that he was hiring staff as others had the hard task of laying people off. Jeff remains busy with Mama Mimi's and can sometimes be found in his basement office at the Clintonville location crunching numbers and thinking of new topping combinations.

TARANTO'S (2000)

Dan Taranto and his younger sister, Debbie, opened Taranto's Pizza Barn on Super Bowl Sunday in 2000. It was in a barn of a former nursery. When Dan worked at Big Bear, he started to think about owning a pizzeria, and after a stint in insurance, it was time to make his dream a reality. He perfected a dough recipe that he was happy with, and the location became a local favorite quickly and earned a top-ten ranking from the *Columbus Dispatch*'s Grumpy Gourmet. Debbie then opened a second Taranto's in the Polaris area but soon found that she had to make adjustments. Unlike the hometown crowd in Pickerington, new Columbus transplants around Polaris were looking for more than just a Columbus-style pizza. It took months to perfect a New York–style pizza recipe but now the location has plenty of variety to please all palates. Both locations focus on high-quality ingredients and plenty of support with their local high schools.

SPARANO'S (2001)

Steven Hill opened Sparano's Pizza in 2001. The Columbus location has moved several times since then, finally landing on Trabue Road, sandwiched between a bar and a gaming shop. Although popular in the area, the pizzeria has largely stayed off the radar, other than pizza-loving Facebook groups. This is surprising since Sparanos has won first, second and third place multiple times at the Slice of Columbus competition. The awards take up a lot of space on the pizzeria's walls. The pizzas offered are definitely crowd pleasers. The Heavy Meat Pizza features layers of pepperoni, ham, ground beef and sausage with extra cheese. The Heavy Duty Pizza is piled with pepperoni, sausage, ham, mushrooms, green peppers, banana peppers and extra cheese. A non-pizza item that has been popular is the Michael Angelo Sub. It has multiple layers of Italian meats on a perfectly toasted bun. Hill

Sparano's Heavy Duty Pizza.

MR. HILL GOES TO THE HILL

Stephen Hill has not drawn much attention to himself or his business since opening Sparano's Pizza in 2001. In 2017, he wrote a letter to Ohio senator Sherrod Brown. In the letter, Hill outlined concerns he had about the disappearing middle class and issues of small businesses. The letter struck a chord with Brown, and he invited Hill to join him as his guest for the State of the Union address. Hill took a well-deserved day off and made the trip to D.C.

---

makes his own dough in house. The business also does a lot to support schools and churches in the surrounding community. The pizza boxes have the "Secret of San Margherita" stamped on them. This is because Sparanos is located in the old San Margherita neighborhood, which was originally a home for early Italian immigrants.

BONO PIZZA (2004–18, MORE OR LESS)

When Bill Yerkes was born, they broke the mold and then smoked it. Eclectic, counterculture, wild, eccentric, unorthodox, erratic and more cannot begin to describe him. Yerkes was a traditional purist (mostly) about one thing: pizza. Yerkes lived in Italy for several years and was turned on to traditional pizza and wood fired ovens. When he eventually came to central Ohio, he started making ovens and pizzas.

Bill quickly became the darling of the Grumpy Gourmet when he started slinging pizza pies in a gas station parking lot. The original BonoPIZZA began in the village of Kilbourne and closed in May 2006 to become Amatos Woodfired Pizza.

The summer of 2008 was the season for Bono Pizza in the Short North. The unconventional ways of pizza purist Bill Yerkes meshed a traditional approach to pizza (well kind of) with many nontraditional elements, such as a unique partnership with a Short North bakery, Eleni Christina, in a location along an alley. The enterprise should not have worked, but it did. In fact, it prospered. It was the darling of Short North and Victorian Village residents and an unofficial meeting point for Columbus Underground ilk.

Bono Pizza. *Courtesy Bethia Woolf/Columbus Food Adventures.*

There were a few chairs inside, a few small patio tables outside and a simple sign on the sidewalk. You could BYOB if everyone agreed to look the other way. The pizza was fantastic. However, like any burning sun, it was bound to extinguish, and it did in the fall of 2008. The deal Yerkes worked out was that he would use the kitchen at night when the bakery was not at work, and he would clear out by the time they needed to knead their own dough. Bill might have overstayed his welcome. The scale might have been tipped by a customer who made Bill add White Castle sliders to a pizza.

There were attempts at rebirth. Bill came full circle with a location near his home at a site vacated by Cowtown Pizza. Showing his very unconventional side and some significant out-of-the-box thinking, Bill used Columbus Underground as a means to raise some fast cash to get his operation going.

Bill put together a proposal for his loyal customers to help raise the extra cash quickly. He called it the BonoPIZZA Pay it Forward Plan, and Bono began selling half-price gift certificates in $100 and $200 increments. The $100 gift certificate cost $50, and the $200 gift certificate cost $100, making it a great deal for anyone planning on dining at Bono in the future. The goal was to sell seventy-five of these certificates to cover the cost of raising the additional $5,000 needed to open. Yerkes met his goal, and no pizzeria materialized.

As a result, most of 2009 was a year without Bono, so the natives started to get a little restless. (The author was one of the people who invested or donated, depending on your perspective, money into BonoBucks gift certificates.) Eventually, a new location was secured in a convenience store across the street from Bill's abode on Northwest Boulevard. Bill had the best commute to work in the local restaurant trade.

The wood fired oven was a centerpiece of the small space, and much of the eating was outside. The always-entertaining personality and styling of Bill Yerkes was somewhat tempered by his saintly wife, Peggy, who was there most evenings to take orders and care for customers. Bill and Peggy were good friends with the Grumpy Gourmet. The Grump's favorite dish, other than Bono Pizza, was the pasta carbonara that Bill made. When Peggy became the caretaker for the Grump and his wife, Bill would come over to prepare the meal.

Bill acquired an apprentice, Jake Wilch, while he was at Northwest Boulevard. Toward the end of the lifespan of the convenience store Bono, Jake became the full-time owner, and Bill faded into the sunset, so to say. Mirroring his mentor, there was a bit of a hiatus between locations. When the new location launched, there were some fears that it would sink, but Jake persevered and "pizzaed" on.

It is hard to describe the Bono experience to non-consumers. The whole was definitely greater than the sum of the parts. Bohemian does not fully reflect the spirit of the place, but a new term I thought of comes close: Bono-hemian: "having informal and unconventional social habits" but formal training and intense passion in the art of pizza production. Jake set up in an apartment complex. His pizza oven was outside. His neighbor was a bar that was connected to his place on one side and Cowtown Pizza on the other. Two pizza places yards apart, of course, it is Bono Pizza. Jake kept the operation going until January 2018. Yerkes passed away in 2020.

SUSIE'S SUB SHOP (2005)

Susie's Sub Shop does have great subs. It also has really good pizza. The origins of the business go back to 1959 and the former D&M Pizza at Weber and Westerville Roads. Denny Hartsell took over, and his friend Charles Bateman came on board as a partner in the early 1970s, after retiring from Western Electric. When Denny died, Bateman took over as full owner with

Customer photo collection at Susie's Sub Shop.

his family. When Charles died, his son John took over the business. The shop closed around 2000. In 2005, the former Rofini's Pizza on Weber Road became available, and the family decided to take over the location and bring Susie's back. In the past, the shop did offer pizza, but it was very much a sideline to the subs. Taking over Rofini's, the family knew they would have to bring their A game for pizza because the community was accustomed to having great pizza from the Rofini's spot.

Susie's moved to a new location on Karl Road in January 2019, when the old B&B Pizza & Spaghetti space became available. Susie's has always been in the Linden area, so it has a longtime following. The business buys from Auddino's Bakery and sources locally as much as possible. The front counter and nearby area are nearly encased with photos that family and customers have added over the years. This was a tradition started years ago and continues this day. A non-pizza item that is a big hit is the Big John Sub, named after John Bateman, who "liked to eat big." The sandwich is a very meaty Italian sub with the addition of a long grilled Italian sausage split in half and placed on top. The business is currently run by a nephew who was also a longtime employee, with some help from Molly Bateman.

Yellow Brick Pizza (2009)

After opening in 2009, Yellow Brick Pizza quickly established itself as a hot spot with good pizza and a craft beer collection with depth and breadth. The owners, Bobby Silver and Faith Pierce, were early pioneers, staking claim to a former laundromat near boarded-up buildings on Oak Street in Olde Town East. These pathfinders led the way for the block to grow a bakery, a bar and some other new businesses. The pizza is described as East Coast style with Rhode Island influences, since one of the owners worked in a few Rhode Island pizza shops. Rhode Island pizza is defined as rectangular baked dough covered with thicker, tomato sauce. It has a thicker crust than most pizzas—but thinner than New York– or Sicilian-style pizzas. Yellow Brick's pizzas are round, but there is a Rhode Island influence.

The dough is hand stretched with a medium thickness to the crust and a signature thick dough ring. For the non-traditional eater, Yellow Brick offers plenty of gluten and vegan friendly options for pizzas, including gluten-free crust, vegan cheese and textured vegetable protein sausage. Its Rhode Island Red sauce adds a bit of heat and kick.

The brick-walled bohemian pizzeria mixes eclectic music, movies instead of sports on TV and portraits of Mexican artist Frida Kahlo and former mayor Mike Coleman. The artist is Bobby Silver.

Yellow Brick opened a second location in Victorian Village in 2018, with a third intended for Franklinton in 2020.

Tristano's Deep Dish at Yellow Brick

If you have the time, seek out the Tristano's Deep Dish Pizza at Yellow Brick. Tristano's deep dish has a thick, braided crust at the ends. The inside is compressed with thick layers of cheese, five to six layers of pepperoni, a sauce with thick and rich tomato sauce and a dough that is chewy. It is among the best Chicago-style pies in central Ohio. The name comes from Tristano's Pizza in Grove City. The pizzeria closed in 2018, but before closing, Yellow Brick asked owner Lou Tristano to teach them how to make his much-loved Chicago pie. Tristano was a glass blower by trade but had a deep love of pizza and cooking. He came from a family of pizza makers in Chicago and started working at his family's pizzeria at an early age. The food at Tristano's was consistently good. The downside with Tristano's was—and Lou would

Tristano's Deep Dish Pizza, the inspiration for Tristano's Chicago Stuffed Pizza at Yellow Brick Pizza.

be the first to admit it—the business side of a restaurant was not his forte, and sometimes his demeanor did not entice staff to stick around. The author was a frequent visitor to Tristano's, and based on eating there many times, the Yellow Brick version of Tristano's Chicago style pie is about 91 percent true to form. Two missing elements are that Tristano's sauce was a bit different, and Lou made his own sausage. Tristanos is missed, especially the Screaming Tristano Pizza, featuring multiple meats and giardiniera. Since Yellow Brick is making Tristano's deep dish correctly, plan to wait at least forty minutes when you place your order. Any true Chicago deep dish will take that long to cook properly.

CLEVER CROW PIZZA (2009–12)

Clever Crow was with us for far too short of a time. It was by far the most different pizza in the history of Columbus. Gary Robinette had a food

Clever Crow Pizza with signature cornbread crust. *Courtesy of Bethia Woolf/Columbus Food Adventures.*

science degree from Ohio State University and learned the pizza making trade while working at a pizzeria in Portland. He used the finest-quality ingredients he could find and shopped as local as possible. What made the pizza memorable and distinctive was the cornbread-style dough and crust. Another remarkable aspect of Clever Crow was where the business started— inside a bar called Circus in the Short North.

Examples of toppings included house-made sausage with a hint of wine, house-made pork-ish pancetta, tasso ham, Canadian bacon, house-pickled vegetables and a good amount of corn.

Clever Crow was so well thought of that it was profiled in a voiceover appearance by Anthony Bourdain for a *No Reservations* episode in 2010. Bourdain did not visit himself, but his film crew loved the pizza. The fame helped Gary Robinette and Brooke Howell move the pizzeria to the North Market, where it had a good run until December 2012.

LATE NIGHT SLICE (2009)

In the early days of Mikey's Late Night Slice, diners could expect a few questions when talking about the pizza. The typical lead question when asking someone if they have had Late Night Slice was "drunk or sober?" The second question was "did you have the Slut Sauce?" Things have changed a bit since then. Mikey is Mike Sorboro. He was carting people around in pedicabs when they were all the rage in the Short North. Most of his rides were late at night, and a fair number of his customers were intoxicated. After being asked countless times where a person could find a slice of pizza late at night, the light bulb, or something, clicked in his head. He rented an old shed in the Short North and started to acquire what was needed to start the business. He and partners Jason Biundo and Bryce Ungerott watched every video they could find on making pizza on YouTube. They also bought all of the pizza dough from both Trader Joe's in town to test recipes.

They opened on Fourth of July weekend in 2009 to a steady business. The first pizzas came from elsewhere and were reheated. Then they started showing old movies on the outside wall opposite of the shack. This and the smell of pizza got people's attention. Business started to pick up, and they started to make their own pizza. It took a while for it to get good. They also entertained customers with irreverent fourth-grade humor. (Today, it is definitely at the eleventh-grade level.)

Their next move was to start one of the first food trucks in the city. Mobile food regulations were a bit hazy at the time, so they bent a few rules to make the truck work. Street parking for food trucks was not legal, but a business allowed them access to a valet parking space. Beat cops might have looked the other way for several years, since feeding drunk people late at night and having an alternative to White Castle at three o'clock in the morning makes for a better life for a third-shift police officer. Mikey's Late Night Slice Food Truck was dubbed a Pizza Assault Vehicle and was an instant hit. The next move was to add another truck and grow the business.

The owners started to establish partnerships with bars and venues around town that needed a food option. They closed several of these partnerships after a few years, but one of the first partnerships, with Ledo's in Old North Columbus, continued until March 2020 (COVID-19 closure).

What they learned serving pizza in bars is that there is a lot more money to be made from drinks than dough. So, they started to work on a Late Night Slice with a bar. The first to open was right next door to their shack. They opened the Oddfellows Bar in 2014. The pizza was still served from the

Brendon Parsh, longtime employee and manager at Late Night Slice.

shack, which was later replaced by a shipping container. They followed with the South Fourth Street location in 2015, which was a full-service bar and Late Night Slice. They took everything they learned about pizza and bars and applied their lessons to their newest bar and Late Night Slice at High and Vine, which opened in 2018. Since it is Late Night Slice, it also includes a secret speakeasy bar in the basement.

Late Night Slice serves New York–style pizza. Over time, it has incorporated the critical elements of a New York slice—high gluten flour, a big crust ring and a bit of attitude. Late Night Slice is renowned for its specialty pizzas and collaborations, including Nashville-style hot chicken on pizza, in collaboration with Hot Chicken Takeover, and a BBQ pizza with Ray Rays. Interesting offerings include Cheezus Crust, two slices of pizza with American cheese pressed together to make a sandwich, and the Rad Vegan, with mushrooms, banana peppers, basil and vegan cheese (animal free). It also does a weekly pizza special, which frequently jumps the shark, including a slice so hot that you have to sign a waiver to eat it.

Biundo, the chief creative officer of the company, has a lighthearted approach to marketing. The Late Night Slice Memes have received national attention from the likes of *PMQ Pizza Magazine*. They sometimes toe the line of legality, but the cease and desist letters have been few and far between over the years

A signature item from Late Night Slice was originally called Slut Sauce. The concept started late one night in the shack. The gang had been experimenting with dipping sauces. They ended up mixing ranch, hot sauce, barbecue sauce and sriracha sauce as the initial recipe. It found its way into a squirt bottle, and eventually, a photo of Paris Hilton was taped on, and a tradition was born. Customers could not get enough of it, and so many customers were pocketing the bottles that the Late Night Slice crew started to bottle it for sale at the shops. The Slut Sauce name came from Sorboro's experiences working at different clubs. Knowing that Paris Hilton could sue them out of existence, that photo disappeared and was replaced by a series of labels over time, which included Nina West before she was nationally known. As the collective sense of humor evolved over time, it was decided to change the name. Many people had complained about the term over the years, and that was a concern. Another issue was the plan to start selling the sauce in stores. For a brief time, they followed the lead of Prince and just used a symbol (Infamous Sauce). Since 2015, it has been called Unicorn Sauce, although longtime Late Night Slice fans will always call it Slut Sauce.

Most people are not aware of the group's long commitment to community events, including Columbus's annual Pride Parade, and well as donating to area nonprofits, such as Toys for Tots and the Doo Dah Parade. They even started their own nonprofit in 2014, the Columbus Diaper Bank, which donates hundreds of thousands of diapers a year to Columbus's neediest families.

While the tone of Late Night Slices humor has ruffled some feathers over the years, the company culture is definitely progressive and respectful.

An incident involving one of their Pizza Assault Trucks made national news in January 2013. Two men were holding hands while waiting in line for pizza. Another man in line started to aggressively harass them with homophobic language. Everyone else in line told him his words were not OK. Then the Late Night Slice employees leaned out of the truck and told him that he would not be served. One of the two men, Joel Diaz, wrote a Facebook post about the incident, and it went viral in less than twenty-four hours. Late Night Slice started selling shirts with the phrase "No Slut Sauce for You, Mr. Homophobe," with a portion of the proceeds going to Equality Ohio, a nonprofit organization that advocates for LGBT families. It might have not been expected from a place that sold Slut Sauce, but Mikey's Late Night Slice has done a lot of unexpected things, including being very successful.

Tyler's Pizza and Bakery (2010)

Bryan Tyler is passionate about baking. He started working at Thurn's Bakery in 1994, when it was a scratch bakery. He then moved on to Great Harvest Bread Company for about five years. His next move was in 2003, when Omega Artisan Bakery was starting at the North Market. Taking the lessons that he learned helping Omega with launching and his previous bakery jobs, Tyler decided to open Bread Basket Family Bakery in Gahanna in 2004. His focus has always been on quality natural ingredients, local and organic when possible, and using sustainable foods with no GMOs or pesticides.

In 2010, he opened a location in Reynoldsburg, and got the wood fired oven that he had wanted for a long time. This allowed him to make pizzas the way he wanted to, and Tyler's Pizzeria and Bakery was born. Pizzas are available in the late afternoon, and baked goods and breads are available all day. The crust is made simply, with white organic flour, salt, yeast and water. No eggs, sugar or oil are used. He also makes his pizza sauce from scratch, using fresh tomatoes, garlic, oregano, basil, salt, black pepper, olive oil and bay leaves. Several interesting specialty pizzas are offered, including the Sunny-Side Up, topped with hand-shredded mozzarella, black forest ham, shredded potatoes, cheddar cheese and sunny-side eggs.

Borgata Pizza (2010)

Borgata was a novelty when it opened in 2010. A friend of the owners had a retail space in need of a purpose on Parkville Road near SR 161 and Cleveland Avenue. This is about the last place in town someone would expect a New York–style pizza place. Borgata is tucked in a retail strip by a service road just west of Cleveland Avenue. It was a tough spot for the food trade. This part of north Columbus had its culinary heyday in the 1980s. The chain restaurants of the area were replaced with the presence of some new ethnic gems and plenty of taco trucks. Borgata is tucked in a retail strip by a service road just west of Cleveland Avenue. As for pizza, most of the people in the area had been eating Massey's Pizza just down the road for a lifetime.

Owner Roz Auddino was familiar with the area—it was not too far from DeSales High School, which he had attended. He spent most of his time working construction before teaming up with Ed Bisconti. Bisconti came to the pizzeria with some culinary chops. A Youngstown native, Bisconti graduated from Johnson and Wales University with a degree in culinary arts and plenty of restaurant experience. The goal was to make Italian food and New York–style pizza using the highest-quality local and regional ingredients available. They continue to make all pastas, pizza dough, sauces, house specialties, vinaigrette salad dressings and desserts from scratch.

The name Borgata loosely translates to "village" and sometimes refers to a neighborhood on the outskirts of an Italian town. Borgata started to draw New York–style pizza fans from all over town as word of mouth spread about a place that could make a proper slice. Local baker and former pizza maker Matt Swint and his friend Dom Rotolo, of Rotolo's Pizza, dub Borgata as the closest thing to a mom-and-pop pizza place in Columbus in the last decade. The growing following prompted a second, bigger and fancier Borgata Pizza in Linworth in 2017. In 2020, a third location was planned for the Budd Dairy Food Hall. The business has come a long way from its beginning.

Harvest Pizzeria (2011)

Chris Crader brought a lot of experience to the table when he opened the first Harvest Pizza in German Village in 2011. Crader had bartending and management experience at Barrio, Due Amici and other restaurants and was well versed in the art and science of serving the public. Harvest was an immediate hit, blending wood fired Neapolitan pies with farm-to-table toppings, finely crafted cocktails, delectable salads, a large selection of small plates and homemade desserts. Some of the produce came from Crader's small farm in Canal Winchester. Harvest is part of the Crader Grow Restaurant Group, which opened other Harvest Pizzeria in Clintonville, Dublin, Bexley and beyond, as well as other concepts. (In 2020, the focus changed to just the Harvest locations.) The Harvest location in German Village, with the complementing Curio craft cocktail bar, remained the fan favorite in the group until it closed in April 2019. While some of the pizza combinations at Harvest are traditional, most are progressive, such as the Spicy Yuma Pizza, featuring a gouda and Havarti blend, mozzarella, chorizo, jalapeños, corn, roasted red pepper and chipotle-spiked tomato sauce.

As an interesting side note, Crader noticed during his long career that bars and restaurants wash a lot of glassware. He started to look for an ecologically sound cleaning agent that worked well and would not streak glasses but could still peel lipstick off a rim. After not finding what he was looking for, he teamed up with Ohio State University to find the right solution, and he did. Today, the product is doing its job.

MEISTER'S PIZZA (2011)

Meister's Pizza is located in a bar that was voted one of the top-ten dive bars in the country by Yelp. The original concept was called Pi Pizza. That was not a typo—not pie like you eat but pi, as in the mathematical concept. The pizza place was created to keep the bellies of hard-drinking, PBR–loving customers sustained through the night. Pi went right over their heads, so since everyone called it Meister's Pizza anyway, they ran with that. The creator of Pi has long since left town, but the legacy remains in the phone number—it ends 3141.

Meister's offers a fine thin crust pizza, a very good French bread pizza and some extra tasty subs. The standout item is the Chicago deep-dish pie. Two of the large, thick slices are enough to fill up even the largest of lumberjacks. The deep-dish approach works in reverse order to the typical laying of pizza. It uses a dough base, followed by toppings, cheese and then sauce—lots of sauce, usually a half inch or so. This sweet-and-spicy tomato mash is infused with strong dumpings—not dashes—of herbs and spices. The crust end or

Meister's Deep Dish Pizza. *Courtesy of Angelo Signorino Jr.*

E, the longtime Sunday-only pizza maker at Meisters, in action.

butt or ring, whatever you might call it, is crisp on the outside, chewy on the inside and about three inches high.

The bar has plenty to entertain if you dine in. It offers a lot of value-priced beverages, and there are plenty of canned and bottled beers, as well as six taps of craft beer. There is a great collection of rock-and-roll memorabilia on the walls, spanning from the 1950s to today. Elvis, Bowie, Foo Fighters fans and everyone in between will find something to spy. The items are part of a massive collection shared by co-owner Matt Meister and his dad. The bar is also an official Browns Backers Bar and is always filled to capacity for home games. Male patrons should take a moment to check out the shower curtain door in the men's bathroom.

Many people order the pizza for carryout. If you do, budget at least an hour if not more on Fridays and Saturdays, and if a crowded bar makes you claustrophobic, come early in the evening.

Natalie's Coal Fired Pizza (2012)

When the trend in Columbus was going the wood fired route, the owners of Natalie's zigged instead of zagged by going with a coal-fired pizza oven. Although uncommon in Ohio (it was believed that Natalie's had the only coal-fired pizza oven in the state), these ovens are commonplace in New York City. Owner Natalie Jackson discovered this spin on pizza in the Big Apple and was determined to bring it to Columbus. She teamed up with her dad, Charlie, to open the restaurant in Worthington. They also incorporated their passion for music, making the space a music venue after 9:00 p.m. The approach to Neapolitan-style pizza is traditional. The crust is slightly charred, they use San Marzano tomatoes and sliced mozzarella and some common Italian toppings, such as goat cheese and sopraffina ricotta. They do get a little funky with the other toppings. While the space is small, the Jacksons got inspired with the basement space, creating a special speakeasy called the Light of the Seven Matchsticks. The space features highly crafted cocktails and a secret menu, and guests are asked to leave their cell phones, children and inhibitions behind.

Fans of the business were thrilled when a second location was opened in Grandview on King Avenue in 2019. The space is three times bigger, so it can host a wider variety of musical acts and a bigger menu.

GoreMade Pizza (2016)

Pizzaiolo Nick Gore had a lot of practice before opening GoreMade Pizza in 2016. His first job was in a pizza shop and his second job too. He then worked with Alana Shock at her eponymous restaurant. This is where Gore developed a passion for local and fresh ingredients. He decided to combine his newfound appreciation for sustainable foods and pizza. At first, he started by having Sunday pizza nights with friends as he developed his recipes and techniques. Then he mounted a wood fired pizza oven on a trailer, making the rounds at farmers markets and catering and pop-up events. He soon developed a following that was nearly as loyal as his Sunday night focus groups for his Neapolitan-style pizzas.

His next step was getting a small storefront in Italian Village, where he spent the next year and a half building out the place. GoreMade Pizza opened in September 2016.

GoreMade is a bit of a play on *gourmet*. Nick does have a gourmet approach to ingredients, but his vision of GoreMade goes well beyond what he puts on the plate. Nick, the maestro of pizzas, has created something at GoreMade that exemplifies the concept of a whole being greater than the sum of the parts.

Nick Gore working the oven at GoreMade Pizza.

At some subconscious level, Nick has created an atmosphere that provides a *Cheers* vibe. They may not always know your name, but they are very glad you came. Conversation flows between those on both sides of the counter. GoreMade tends to act as a magnet for people who like to talk about food almost as much as they like to eat it. The conversations don't just stick to making pizzas; you are just as likely to talk about making patios, figuring out how to make a charcuterie board with some foraged black walnut or how to connect with the community. Guests come in to hang out as much as to dine. Some might opt to have a drink on the patio after a pizza, while others might bond while playing a board game at the bar.

GoreMade food is not fully focused on being only artisan and avant-garde; Nick is a craftsman as well. He built much of what is in the space with materials often sourced from friends and family. The wood-fired oven, which goes by the name of Ferdinand, has received nods of approval from practitioners in New York and Naples alike. The size and shape of the oven limits mass production of pizzas, and he can do about two at a time at full speed. However, what is missing in quantity is made up in quality. The oven maintains a steady, consistent temperature without wasting any wood. Nick coaxes out a bit extra from each crust and flavor, with his attention to detail and eye for ingredient pairings.

At GoreMade, guests can choose their own adventure. You can order safe, sensible and traditional dishes or take a journey and see where it leads you. Either way, you will feel the spirit of the space among the community of people who care about what they eat and who they eat with at the counter.

In the back corner, a black dry-erase board lists salads and specials focused on local and seasonal ingredients. As a general rule, if something is currently growing, it will appear somewhere on the menu. Butternut squash is a frequent and popular item. Meats, cheeses and root vegetables take over the menu in the winter. Every trip to GoreMade is an adventure.

PAULIE GEE'S (2016)

In New York City, specifically Brooklyn, where residents are particular about their pizzas, Paulie Gee's is held in high regard. Its approach to pizza is traditional with a modern twist. The mission of Paulie Gee's was to expand, and any business that wants to go national will come calling to

Pizza oven at Paulie G's in the Short North. *Courtesy of Bethia Woolf/Columbus Food Adventure.*

Columbus. In 2016, it opened a location in the Short North in partnership with Terry Gibbs.

The spot brings Neapolitan-style pies created in a wood-burning Stefano Ferrara oven and a bar with a deep selection of local beers and wine. It combines Paulie G's core menu and new creations by Gibbs. Gibbs spent a year at the New York Paulie Gee's making sure that everything that was good about Paulie Gee's could be replicated in Columbus.

Our Paulie Gee's has localized the menu with a few tributes to culinary Columbus. For example, the Katzingers (Swiss, pastrami, post-oven sauerkraut with Russian dressing drizzle) and the Hog Pit Brisket Fresh Mozzarella (Ray Ray's Hog Pit BBQ beef brisket, pickled red onion and

Ray Ray's BBQ sauce). Going way out of the region, Paulie Gee's has added what many consider to be the best Detroit-style pizza in the city, if not the state. Fans of New York–style pizza will not be disappointed, Paulie G's serves a slice that even a New Yorker will enjoy.

FIBONACCI PIZZERIA (2020)

When Studio 35 finally completed its long-awaited second floor remodel, there was much rejoicing. It was not just a second screen with recliner seating that won praise but also the addition of food. Studio 35 has kept guests fed with pizza brought in from its pizza shop neighbor for years, but the addition provided enough room for Fibonacci's Pizzeria. The name is a tribute to Leonardo de Pisa, the Italian mathematician who created the Fibonacci sequence/golden ratio. The oven is from Maryland and was built on-site. The volcanic stones for the oven were imported from Italy. The interior rack rotates, and a seven-hundred-degree temperature allows the pizzas to cook in two minutes. The goal is to source as locally and seasonally as possible, with partnerships including Ezzo Sausage and Good Food Bakery. Pizza purists will be happy to know that the dough is made with 00 flour, water, salt and yeast. There are no added sugars or oils.

The guy calling the shots at the oven is Gabe Sturgess. Sturgess has been with the theater for over twenty years as a bartender and the caregiver to the ancient geothermal heating and cooling system, along with plenty of other jobs. His key to sourcing some of the great beers at the bar was one of his many other side jobs: he has been a brewer at Barley's for many years. He is now replacing the hops he grew on the second-floor deck with herbs.

Fibonacci's Pizzeria is a perfect fit for its home. The building opened as the Indianola Theater in 1938. It was then the Marzetti Theater (owned by Frank Marzetti). The Studio 35 name comes from the 35mm film that was used in the projectors. In 1972, the theater was the first in the United States to get permission to serve alcohol. Longtime owner John Conti kept the theater going with double features of second-run movies and a lot of creative programming. The current owners, Eric Brembeck and Rita Volpi, took over and worked hard to save the theater, which is the last independent theater in Columbus. They built a bar that gained a reputation as one of the best craft beer bars in the city. They also feature special beer tasting events paired with movies, including their perennially sold-out Dudeathon, which features the Big Lebowski.

Care for a supernatural side with your movie or meal? Studio 35 might also be one of the most haunted spots in the city. The following are some examples:

- There is a ghost who is an older man who wears a bowler hat and appears to be dressed in 1910- or 1920-era clothes. Paranormal investigators visited the movie theater and found high electromagnetic readings on the preferred seat of the ghost, whose name, they discovered, is Charlie. Also, a couple from the 1930s has been sighted.
- A dog was shot during a break-in at the upstairs apartment. The dog's name is Tora, and it still shows up to the theater. Sturgess has seen the dog in his time at the theater, and it scared the saffron out of him.
- A man in a military uniform is often spotted walking around.
- Workers heard a young girl crying in the bathroom when doing the bar remodel.
- Photos of dead children were found upstairs during a renovation.
- In the 1970s, a man died in the auditorium.

MASSEY'S 5.0 (2000–PRESENT)

Jed and Dave Pallone are still deeply involved with Massey's pizza over twenty years since they purchased the business from their cousin in 1999. Keeping the tradition of a family business, they added son-in-law Rich Folk on the marketing side. Dave's son Dominic and Jed's son Nick have taken on day-to-day operational decisions. The Pallones have grown the business to fifteen locations, including one in South Carolina. Massey's has added many new menu items while staying true to the original pizza traditions. The family also started a sports bar pizzeria concept at some locations, which has been very successful. Massey's was among the first chains to offer gluten-free and cauliflower crust.

DONATOS (2000–PRESENT)

By 2003, the McDonatos era was over. Jane Abel (Grote), Jim's daughter, had a vision to return Donatos to a family company. Donatos came back home and took the lessons learned from the corporate experience and blended those with the ideals and principles Jim Grote had developed since 1963. The Grotes learned about expanding a business from McDonald's, but this time, the family would grow the company the Donatos way, with a different customer and employee focus. In 2004, Donatos established a relationship with Kroger to supply take-and-bake pizzas to hundreds of locations. In 2013, Jane was on an episode of the television show *Undercover Boss*. As of 2020, Donatos had over 160 locations, with an eye on growth in Florida and west of the Mississippi, as well as a partnership with Red Robin Restaurants.

NAPICS (2003–16)

The North American Pizza and Ice Cream Show (NAPICS) took over the Columbus Convention Center for two days every winter from 2003 to 2016. It was the second-largest pizza-focused trade show in the country. The event showcased anything a pizzeria or ice cream shop owner would need to run their business. And there were plenty of free samples of meats, cheeses, topping and ice cream offered to all attendees. Visitors would leave with plenty of swag. For pizzerias, they could see and try out everything from ovens to new brands of pepperoni. There were numerous competitions, as well, including the event that was known as Pizza Pizzazz. Contests ranged from best-of competitions for different styles of pizza to dough tossing. Competitions and demonstrations featured nationally known pizza celebrities, pizza shop owners from across the country and culinary students. The show was replaced by the Mid-America Restaurant expo in 2017, which continues to have a significant number of pizza-focused vendors.

PIZZA WHISKEY

If there was ever a community that would embrace a pizza whiskey, it would be Columbus. And if there was ever a distiller to concoct it, that would be

Pizza Pie Chuga from 451 Spirits with a slice of Late Night Slice Pizza *Courtesy of Chad Kessler of 451 Spirits.*

Chad Kessler. Kessler is a counterculture renaissance man. In addition to skateboarding, surfing Lake Erie and playing in a band, he distills spirits. His training ground for the craft was Weiland's Market, where, as he says, he was able to drink above his pay grade in his five years working the beer and spirits department. Inspired by the work, he found his way to distilling at 451 Spirits, a small space in a former car wash that is next to a bar and behind a convenience store. Kessler's approach to distilling is both traditional and unconventional at the same time. He is not one to follow the trends—any of them—but one day, he had an inspiration. Kessler is fond of Mexican spirits. One he found very intriguing was mezcal de pechuga. One of the unique elements of the alcohol involves hanging a chicken breast over the open vat while distilling. This cooks the chicken and is believed to add a unique flavor to the spirit.

Kessler also likes pizza. On a whim, he decided he would make a pizza whiskey. After some trial and error, he determined that to get the right balance, he would need to add sundried tomatoes, garlic, basil, parmesan cheese, pepperoni and a piece of Late Night Slice. It turned out better than expected, so he decided to make enough to fill a few cases and see if Late Night Slice might buy some so that he could at least cover the costs of his experiment. Late Night Slice embraced the spirit. Kessler had a few cases to sell at the distillery, and surprisingly, they sold quickly. He was happy to have some fun with his idea and move on to more serious experiments. Then an article came out about his Pizza Pie'Chuga, and the phones started ringing off the hook. The downside was that there was little to none left. Kessler did not want to be known as the pizza whiskey guy out of fear that requests might come to do a White Castle or Hot Chicken Takeover whiskey, but due to demand, he made another batch and then another and another. Demand has decreased a bit, but he still occasionally makes a small batch so that the story can continue. But please don't ask him what other food spirits he might make.

Pizza Boxes

One of the greatest areas of focus in the last fifty years has been improving the ability to get a pizza that is as good as eating in delivered to customers. In the 1940s, carryout pizza was often placed on a sheet of cardboard and then slid into a paper bag. As the pizza delivery business grew, the need to stack pizzas on top of one another became a necessity. Bags did not work, but boxes did. In Columbus, some places started with donut boxes. Many credit Domino's Pizza as the inventor of pizza boxes in the early 1960s. Boxes provide the option to stack multiple pizzas and keep them stable.

There are a lot of downsides to using boxes. The thinner cardstock boxes don't hold up well to pizza grease and are harder to stack and transport than their corrugated cardboard cousins. They also do not retain stamped logos very well. Thick or thin, boxes tend to steam up pizza on the way home. Sometimes the box lid can get soggy and collapse into the pizza or the steam might affect the crust or consistency. This is why Massey's held on to its trademark brown paper bags for so long and why Rubino's still uses them to this day. (They will charge you if you ask for a box.) Companies continue to look for the perfect box for pizza. Innovators look for ways to fine-tune venting, make them easier to recycle, make them biodegradable and protect pizza from the cardboard. In 1988, Pizza Hut adopted what is known as the Chicago Folding Box, which folds together differently. In 2019, Pizza Hut started to test out a round box. The perfect pizza box has not been created yet, but the quest will continue.

8

THE FUTURE OF PIZZA IN COLUMBUS

I n 1950, the path of pizza's preeminence in Columbus started in a small restaurant opened by two friends who both found a similar path to Columbus—a wife. Since then, a large number of small family businesses grew with the city and created a style of pizza that would be a trademark of Columbus. It took a lot of hard work, long nights and the devotion of family and employees to establish pizza as a beloved food in Columbus. Ironically, in a city named in honor of an Italian explorer, it was pizza that first put Columbus on the culinary map and placed a spotlight on our tight-knit Italian American community.

Many of these pizzerias started as second businesses. Often working nights and weekends, immigrant entrepreneurs were able to grow their own businesses while keeping their day jobs. There are countless second-, third- and fourth-generation families in pizza shops around Columbus. There are so many great traditions that link these pizza parlors to families throughout the city.

However, after more than seventy years, the legacy of a mom-and-pop pizza shop is fading. Pizza is considered to be the most competitive segment of the food business, with the number of corporate and franchise operations continuing to grow and the number of independent pizzas on a steady decline. What does the future look like for pizza in Columbus?

Two things are certain: Donatos will continue to grow, and Columbus will probably continue to consume copious amounts of pepperoni.

For the longtime mom-and-pop shops, the owners were faced with more pressure from corporate chains. What affects every pizza business is the change of demographics. For many years, Columbus had more pizzerias per capita than any other city in the country. Since those days, our city and our culinary choices have diversified. Current lists show Columbus as either ninth or past fiftieth in pizzeria rankings. While the chains continue to grow, the old-school pizzerias have largely stuck with one or two locations. Several that expanded to five or more locations in the previous decades have scaled back to one or two locations in the last few years. The challenges of training and retaining workers, the costs of healthcare benefits if you have more than a certain number of full-time employees and the rising cost of ingredients cut deeply into any profit margin. Large chains can better control costs by buying in massive quantities and tend to use lower-end ingredients.

Many pizza shops are sustained by families in the neighborhood who have bought from them for generations. As Columbus spreads out and new people move in, the local affinity and loyalty to the neighborhood spot is diffused. More and more people opt to order a pizza online and have it delivered by a third party. This cuts the connection between the pizza maker and the pizza eater. The increasingly common dynamic of a third-party delivery also often cuts into the profit per pizza. Interacting with a constantly changing delivery driver at the counter is not the same as seeing the same person drop in week after week over the years. It might seem like a small thing, but most pizzeria owners enjoy having a personal connection to their customers and community. Many of our "heritage" pizza shops have employees who have worked twenty, thirty or even forty years for the same family. It is unlikely that anyone new to a pizzeria today will still be there two years later and even less likely that they'll be there in two decades. Our culture and community have changed and so has pizza as we knew it. The first pizza a person eats tends to imprint what pizza should be. With more and more people having their first pizza from a chain, that first imprint is likely to stick, especially since chains provide multiple locations to eat their product and can quickly pop up where the masses are moving.

The dynamics of family businesses have changed, as well. Smaller families mean smaller in-house workforces and fewer candidates to assume ownership in the next generation. Many growing up in the business opt for something else after high school or college. In most businesses, it is rare to survive past a second generation. Some pizzerias have made it to the fourth generation, but the number of businesses with ownership succession to family members has decreased.

Pizza has changed too. It is no longer a novelty or "exotic" cuisine. It can be found everywhere. Too many frozen pizza brands to count at the grocery store, a flatbread on countless menus and convenience store pizzas mean pizza has become ubiquitous. Many grocery stores offer take-and-bake pizzas. When pizzerias started, they offered a rare late-night dining option, and today, we have countless twenty-four-hour and late-night choices. Expectations have changed too. Columbus eaters have become promiscuous—with so many choices, they are overloaded with fear of missing out on the newest offering. Heaven forbid eating the same thing two weeks in a row. For dine-in customers, most are not content with a few simple tables and red checkerboard tablecloths; guests want Wi-Fi, multiple TV screens, more food variety and alcohol. And everything, whether dine-in or delivery, should be fast. Customers want a coupon, an app and something different. While pizza remains a comfort food for many, we have a lot more comfort food choices today. As for the desire for something different, consider the rise of gluten-free pizza, cauliflower crust pizza and more.

Few new old-school Columbus-style mom-and-pop shops have opened since the 1990s, and those that we do have are slowly fading away for the reasons listed here.

My hope is that, as you have read the stories in this book, you have found at least one new old place to try or made a special trip to the pizzeria of your youth if you are a Columbus native. The pizzerias in our city offer a culture and tradition that is worthy of preserving, as well as a high dose of calories and carbohydrates.

The COVID-19 Chronicles

This chapter was started before "stay at home" and "COVID" were common terms. At the beginning of the COVID-19 era, most food businesses saw staggering losses. Many pizza places saw a drop in sales, too, but not double-digit percentages like other food businesses. Some pizzerias struggled to stay open while others had their highest sales in history. Those that had a previously strong pickup and delivery businesses saw a large surge in revenue. Those that relied on dine-in sales to lift profit margins took a very big hit. Shops that had a building that was not easy to pick up from struggled to make delivery sufficiently socially distant. Longtime campus landmark Catfish Biff's closed for months, while Adriatico's was

Homemade "0 Capacity" sign at Iacono's Pizza on Kenny Road. COVID-19 shut down its dining room, but it had a brisk carryout business.

able to stay open with easy pickup options and plenty of hungry hospital workers to feed. Old-school businesses like Gatto's and Emelio's jumped into the twenty-first century by adding Instagram accounts. There were shortages of yeast for those that make their own dough and rising prices for meat. RDP, with origins as a supplier to pizzerias in the 1950s, was lucky to have pizzerias still open when the majority of their restaurant and bar customers were closed or doing much less business. During March, April and May 2020, some pizza places were doing 1.5 times their peak business, and a few shut their doors. It was feast or famine, with few in the middle. Only time will tell what long-term effect COVID-19 will have on Columbus pizzerias, but it definitely upped the overall consumption rate for several months in 2020. The upside is that these events made the pizza industry, from large chains to individual mom-and-pop shops, rethink their business models. At the local level, Columbus rediscovered pizza and showed an outpouring of support for local pizza businesses.

BIBLIOGRAPHY

Introduction

Corrova, James. Interview by Jim Ellison. October 18 and 23, 2019.
Pizza Hall of Fame. "Pizzi Cafe." http://pizzahalloffame.com.
Sirij, Laura. Interview by Jim Ellison. January 27, 2020.
Wolf, Barnet D. "Any Way You Slice It—Columbus' Appetite for Pizza." *Columbus Dispatch*, August 25, 2000.

1. Primordial Pizza

Corrova, James. Interview by Jim Ellison. October 18 and 23, 2019.
DiPaolo, Dick, Paul DiPaolo, Mark Mizer, Rita Mizer (DiPaolo) and Norm Mizer. Interview with Jim Ellison. November 23, 2019.
Eal, Ray, Nick Ray and Mark Mizer. Interview by Jim Ellison. July 23, 2019.

2. Pioneers of Columbus Pizza

Massey's

Hayes, Ben. "Around Columbus." *Columbus Citizen*, October 3, 1955.
"Massey's Pizza Holds Grand Opening Today, Sunday." *Lancaster Eagle Gazette*, November 11, 1961.

Massucci, Joseph D. Phone interview by Jim Ellison. December 30, 2019.

Rodgers, Richard. "Cheese, Tomato Pizzas Have a Wide Appeal." *Columbus Citizen*, October 27, 1951.

Sirij, Laura. Interview by Jim Ellison. January 27, 2020.

Waterfield, Mary. "The Man Who Made Pizza." *Columbus Dispatch*, November 22, 1981.

Tommy's

Chenoweth, Doral. "Pizza Honors Go to Tommy's—First Then, First Now." *Columbus Dispatch*, April 20, 1989.

Roesch, Joe. Interview with Jim Ellison. December 11, 2019.

Saulters, Brock. "Tommy's History" e-mail to author, May 29, 2020

Smeltzer, Nancy J. "Thomas Iacono, 78, Dies of Heart Attack." *Columbus Dispatch*, January 4, 1999.

Gatto's

Gatto, Vince. Interview by Jim Ellison. July 11, 2019.

Leonardo's

Ellison, James. "Columbus Pizza History: A Slice by Slice Account." *CMH Gourmand* (blog), October 5, 2008. http://CMHGourmand.com.

Farynowski, Debbie (Grandview Historical Society). Leonardo's Pizza of Grandview. E-mail to author, March 9, 2020.

Humphrey, Latyna M, (Franklin County Auditor's Office). Contact Us Form Submission. E-mail to author, March 4, 2020.

Panzera, Nick. Interview by Jim Ellison. October 17, 2019.

Rubino's

Bloom, Richard E. "Residents Back Pizzeria." *Columbus Dispatch*, April 13, 1983.

Ellison, James. "Rubinos: A Bexley Classic, My Pizza Pilgrimage." *CMH Gourmand* (blog), February 1, 2015. http://CMHGourmand.com.

Greene, Bob. *Be True to Your School: A Diary of 1964*. New York: Scribner, 1987.

3. PILLARS OF PIZZA

American Italian Golf Association

American Italian Golf Association. "Our History." https://www.aigagolf.org.
Rinehart, Earl. "Riviera Country Club to Close." *Columbus Dispatch*, April 6, 2015.

Ritchie DiPaolo/DiPaolo Foods/RDP

Ball, Brian R. "Family Tradition." *Columbus Business First*, July 13, 1998.
DiPaolo, Dick, Paul DiPaolo, Mark Mizer, Rita Mizer (DiPaolo) and Norm Mizer. Interview by Jim Ellison. November 23, 2019.
Smart Business. "Meet the Families." http://www.sbnonline.com.

Italian American Neighborhoods

DiPaolo, Dick, Paul DiPaolo, Mark Mizer, Rita Mizer (DiPaolo) and Norm Mizer. Interview by Jim Ellison. November 23, 2019.
Hambrick, Jennifer. "The Great American Melting Pot: A Walk Through the Past in Italian Village." *Short North Gazette*, December 2005.
Long, Jeff. "Hidden Columbus: Searching for San Margherita." *Columbus Monthly*, November 2019.
"Marble Cliff, Ohio." https://en.wikipedia.org.

4. PIZZA PROLIFERATES

Becker, Lois K. "Pizza Reigns Supreme." *Columbus Sunday Dispatch*, August 11, 1957.

Ange's

Angeletti, Mike, Steve Angeletti and Linda Angeletti. Interview by Jim Ellison. February 3, 2020.

Josie's

Catafina, Wanda. Interview by Jim Ellison. December 27, 2019.

Terita's

Iannarino, Tom. Interview by Jim Ellison. July 3, 2019.

Emelio's

DiSabato, Maria. Interview by Jim Ellison. September 24, 2019.

Pizza House

Ellison, James. "Pizza House Pushing Past the Fifty Year Mark." *CMH Gourmand* (blog), June 20, 2011. http://CMHGourmand.com.
Pizza House. "About." https://www.pizzahousecolumbus.com.

Vick's

Ellison, James. "Vicks Gourmet Pizza Reynoldsburg." *CMH Gourmand* (blog), December 21, 2017. http://CMHGourmand.com.
Vick's Gourmet Pizza. "About Us." https://vicksgourmetpizza.com.

Massey's

Amatos, Christopher A. "Massey's Moves into Franchising—Pizza Chain Aims." *Columbus Dispatch*, December 27, 1993.

Massucci, Joseph D. Phone interview by Jim Ellison. December 30, 2019.

Waterfield, Mary. "The Man Who Made Pizza." *Columbus Dispatch*, November 22, 1981.

Donatos

FundingUniverse. "History of Donatos Pizzeria Corporation." http://www.fundinguniverse.com.

Grote Abel, Jane. *The Missing Piece: Doing Business the Donatos Way*. Columbus, OH: Donatos, 2015.

Pizza Market Place. "Profile: Jim Grote." https://www.pizzamarketplace.com.

Zamarelli's Pizza Palace

Columbus Navigator. "Best Restaurants in Grove City." https://www.columbusnavigator.com.

Zamarellis Pizza Palace. http://www.zamarellispizzapalace.com.

Panzera's

Lombardi, Andy, and Frank Lombardi. Interview by Jim Ellison. October 10, 2019.

Panzera, Nick. Interview by Jim Ellison. October 17, 2019.

Papa Joe's

LaLonde, Brent, and Alice Thomas. "Papa Joes Fire Is Sober News to Fans." *Columbus Dispatch*, April 4, 1996.

Minelli's

Decker, Theodore. "Cops Play Robbers in Police-Recruit Training—Businesses Help Out Academy with Realistic Scenarios." *Columbus Dispatch*, January 27, 2009.

"The Long, Slow Demise of the Delphi Plant." *Columbus Monthly*, December 22, 2014. https://www.columbusmonthly.com.

Joseppi's

Ellison, James. "The Challenge of Joseppis Mega Meat Challenge." *CMH Gourmand* (blog), November 24, 2014. https://cmhgourmand.com.
Joseppi's Pizza. "Our Story, The Passion for Pizza." https://www.joseppispizza.com.

Auddino's

Dominianni, Andy, and Erin Dominianni. *Columbus Italians*. Charleston, SC: Arcadia Publishing, 2011.
Ellison, James. "Auddino's Italian Bakery: Audaciously Awesome Donuts." *CMH Gourmand* (blog), January 2, 2011. https://cmhgourmand.com.
Hooper, Mitch. "Family Ties: Auddino's Italian Bakery." *614 Magazine*, April 30, 2020. https://614now.com.

Ovens

Forno Bravio. "4 Types of Pizza Ovens." https://fornobravodc.com.
Swint, Matt (Matija Breads, former Rotolo's Pizza manager). Interview by Jim Ellison. October 2019.

5. Pizza Preeminence

D&EZO's

Stanley, Greg. Phone interview with Jim Ellison. February 8, 2020.

Eagles

Eagles Pizza. "Welcome to Eagles Pizza." http://eagles-pizza.com.

Johnnies Villa Pizza. "History." http://johnniesvillapizza.com.
Woods, Jim. "Doran Clan Reunites on 1800s Homestead for the 80th Time." *Columbus Dispatch*, August 28, 2005.

Massey's

Ellison, James. "Columbus Pizza History: A Slice by Slice Account." *CMH Gourmand* (blog), October 5, 2008. http://CMHGourmand.com.
Hicks, Randy. Phone interview with Jim Ellison. December 10, 2019.

Dante's

Apollonio, Joe. Interview with Jim Ellison. September 19, 2019.

Rotolo's

Rotolo, Dominc. Interview with Jim Ellison. February 2, 2020.
Wolf, Barnet D. "A Bigger Slice of the Pie." *Columbus Dispatch*, February 26, 2005.

Little Sicily's

Ellison, James. "Little Sicily's Pizza Worth the Drive." *CMH Gourmand* (blog), December 29, 2013. https://cmhgourmand.com.
"Homemade Pizza Is Still 'Worth the Drive.'" *This Week News*, September 30, 2012. https://www.thisweeknews.com.

Flyers

Flyers Pizza. "Our Story." https://www.flyerspizza.com.
Trowbridge, Denise. "Flyers Pizza Holds on to Slice of the Pie." *Columbus Dispatch*, May 3. 2011.

Capuano's

Bracken, Drew. "Capuano's Pizza Serving up Pizza in Pataskala for More Than 40 Years." *Newark Advocate*, December 18, 2018.
Capuanos. "Our Story." https://www.capuanospizza.com.

Iacono's

Chenoweth, Doral. "Daunted Reviewer Is Detoured to Lucky Find." *Columbus Dispatch*, December 6, 1984.

Villa Nova

"A Collection for the Gages." *National Board Bulletin*, 2013.
Villa Nova Riatorante. "About." https://villanovacolumbus.com.

Antolino's Pizza

Snyder, James. Email to author, June 10, 2020.
———. Phone interview by Jim Ellison. February 5, 2020.

Kingy's

Kemper, Kevin. "Kingys' Pizza, Beer and Ribs Make Splash in Small Town." *Columbus Business First*, May 29, 2006.
"Neighborhood Pizza Pub Receives National Recognition." *PMQ Pizza Magazine*, August 2014. https://www.pmq.com.

Bexley Pizza Plus

Rocco, Brad. Interview by Jim Ellison. June 26, 2019.

Catfish Biffs

Youngblood, Nicholas. "The Faces Behind Ohio State's Late Night Restaurants." *Lantern*, December 26, 2018.

Ezzo

Grote Abel, Jane. "The Missing Piece: Doing Business the Donatos Way" Columbus: Donatos, 2015.
Kollker, Blake. "Not Just Any Pepperoni." AzziPizza. November 27, 2017. https://azzippizza.com.
McMillian, J.R. "Going Global: Ezzo's Pepperoni Puts Columbus-Style Pizza on the Map." *614 Magazine*, January 2020.

6. PIZZA PEAKS

Wolf, Barnet D. "Any Way You Slice It—Columbus' Appetite For." *Columbus Dispatch*, August 25, 2000.

Plank's

Clark, John. "Business Spotlight: Pizza Place Now in 3rd Generation." German Village Society. https://germanvillage.com.
McGinnis, John. Phone interview with Jim Ellison. June 15, 2020.
Seman, Gary, Jr. "Columbus' Plank's on Parsons Celebrates 80th Anniversary." *ThisWeek News*, November 16, 2019.

Adriatico's

Ellison, James. "Adriatico's OSU Campus 2.0 Carries on the Legacy of Great Pizza." *CMH Gourmand* (blog), July 7, 2019. https://cmhgourmand.com.
———. "Arrivederci Adriaticos 1.0." *CMH Gourmand* (blog), May 19, 2018. https://cmhgourmand.com.

Enrico's

Tiziana (last name withheld by request). Interview with Jim Ellison. August 20, 2019.

Pasquale's

King, Andrew. "Pasquale's Finds New Home on W. Schrock Road." *ThisWeek News*, July 28, 2015.

Grandad's Pizza

Lovelace, Craig. "Stephen Baumann's Grandad's Pizza on Morse Road Has Used the Same Recipe Since It Opened." *Columbus Business First*, August 31, 2012.
Trowbridge, Denise. "Local Pizza Shops Defend Turf from New Rivals." *Columbus Dispatch*, July 10, 2012.

Figlio

Figlio Pizza. "History Grandview." http://figliopizza.com.
"Laurie & Peter Danis, Owners of Figlio and Vino Vino." *Columbus Monthly*, October 30, 2013. https://www.columbusmonthly.com.
Marshall, John. "Review: Figlio Wood Fired Pizza." *Columbus Monthly*, February 2018.

Hounddogs

Ellison, James. "Hounddogs Debuts New Delivery Vehicle." *CMH Gourmand* (blog), June 1, 2015. https://cmhgourmand.com.
———. "Hounddogs Hallowed Delivery Icon." *CMH Gourmand* (blog), January 18, 2016. https://cmhgourmand.com.
———. "Hounddogs Three Degree Pizza Revisited Reviewed Revived." *CMH Gourmand* (blog), February 28, 2015. https://cmhgourmand.com.

Lost Planet

Ellison, James. "Galaxy Cafe a Story of Passion." *CMH Gourmand* (blog), February 10, 2010. https://cmhgourmand.com.

Benny's

Bennys Pizza. "Our Restaurant." https://bennyspizza.com.
Ellison, James. "Benny's Pizza Marysville." *CMH Gourmand* (blog), April 30, 2011. https://cmhgourmand.com.
Fox 28. "Best Bite Benny's Pizza in Marysville." https://myfox28columbus.com.

Massey's

Amatos, Christopher A. "Massey's Moves into Franchising—Pizza Chain Aims." *Columbus Dispatch*, December 27, 1993.
Pallone, Dave, Jim Pallone and Richard Folk. Interview with Jim Ellison. January 20, 2020.

Donatos

Grote Abel, Jane. *The Missing Piece: Doing Business the Donatos Way*. Columbus, OH: Donatos, 2015.

Slice of Columbus

Shaughnessy, Rebecca. Email to author. May 26, 2020.

St. John's

Millitello, Vince. Phone interview with Jim Ellison. May 22, 2020.

Pizza Saver

Mental Floss. "How Pizza Saver Invention Transformed Pizza Delivery."
  https://www.mentalfloss.com.

Insulated Bag

Koplos, Joanie. "She's Got It 'In the Bag.'" *Sun Day News*, July 3, 2014.

7. Pizza Permutations

Mama Mimi's

Aufdencamp, Jeff. Interview with Jim Ellison. July 8, 2019.

Taranto's

Tarantos Pizza. "About." https://www.tarantospizzeria.com.

Sparano's

Borchers, Laura. "Columbus Pizza Shop Owner Invited to View Presidential
  Address." 10TV.Com, February 28, 2017. https://www.10tv.com.
Ellison, James. "Sparanos the Secret of San Margherita Home of the Heavy
  Duty Pizza." *CMH Gourmand* (blog), January 30, 2011. https://https://
  cmhgourmand.com.

Bono

Ellison, James. "Bedtime for Bono." *CMH Gourmand* (blog), December 11,
  2008. https://cmhgourmand.com.
———. "Bono Pizza." *CMH Gourmand* (blog), December 8, 2017. https://
  cmhgourmand.com.

Susie's

Bateman, Molly. Phone interview with Jim Ellison. September 16, 2019.

Yellow Brick

Ellison, James. "Yellow Brick Pizza and the Old Towne East Intersection." *CMH Gourmand* (blog), June 6, 2016. https://cmhgourmand.com.
———. "Yellow Bricks Tristanos Deep Dish Pizza Test Drive." *CMH Gourmand* (blog), January 15, 2017. https://cmhgourmand.com.

Clever Crow

Ellison, James. "Clever Crow What You Need to Know." *CMH Gourmand* (blog), January 15, 2011. https://cmhgourmand.com.

Late Night Slice

Ellison, James. "Late Night Slice Pizza Box." *CMH Gourmand* (blog), May 29, 2018. https://cmhgourmand.com.
———. "LNS Late Night Slice" *CMH Gourmand* (blog), July 13, 2009. https://cmhgourmand.com.
"We Stayed Up Past Our Bedtime at Mikey's Late Night Slice, Home of Pizzaface, Cheezus Crust and One Very Drunk Mr. Potato Head." *PMQ Pizza Magazine*, January 2017. https://www.pmq.com.
"You'll Laugh. You'll Cry. You'll Drool a Little Bit: 10 Hilarious Pizza Memes from Mikey's Late Night Slice." *PMQ Pizza Magazine*, January 2017. https://www.pmq.com.

Tyler's

Seman, Gary, Jr. "Details Enhance Baker's Pizzas, Breads." *Columbus Dispatch*, November 8, 2018.

Borgata

Budd Dairy Hall. "About Borgata Pizza." Chef Partner Ed Bisconti, Borgata Pizza. https://budddairyfoodhall.com.

Ellison, James. "Borgata Pizza Cafe Story of the Little Guy in the Big CMH Pizza Pie Picture." *CMH Gourmand* (blog), January 15, 2011. https://cmhgourmand.com.

Harvest

Ellison, James. "Harvest Pizza Patio Pleasure." *CMH Gourmand* (blog), September 16, 2011. https://cmhgourmand.com.

Meister's Pizza

Ellison, James. "Quickbyte Be It Pi or Meisters This Pizza Is Pleasing." *CMH Gourmand* (blog), January 30, 2013. https://cmhgourmand.com.

Natalie's

"Natalie's Coal Fired Pizza Opens in Worthington." *Columbus Underground*, August 5, 2012. https://www.columbusunderground.com.

GoreMade

Ellison, James. "GoreMade Pizza a Great Place If You Get It." *CMH Gourmand* (blog), January 2, 2018. https://cmhgourmand.com.

GoreMadePizza. "Our Story." https://goremadepizza.com.

Pizza Today. "On the Road GoreMade Columbus, OH." https://www.pizzatoday.com.

Paulie Gee's

Houck, Brenna. "Paulie Gee First Columbus Ohio Restaurant Pizzeria Opening." *Eater*, January 17, 2016. https://www.eater.com.

Fibonacci Pizzeria

"Studio 35 Expands with Pizzeria Second Screen." Columbus Underground, February 27, 2020. https://www.columbusunderground.com.

Donatos

Grote Abel, Jane. *The Missing Piece: Doing Business the Donatos Way*. Columbus, OH: Donatos, 2015.

Massey's

Pallone, Dave, Jim Pallone and Richard Folk. Interview with Jim Ellison. January 20, 2020.

NAPICS

Ellison, James. "NAPICS Pizza and Ice Cream and Freebies Oh My." *CMH Gourmand* (blog), February 25, 2009. https://cmhgourmand.com.

Pizza Whiskey

451 Spirits. "Limited Releases." https://www.451spirits.com.

Boxes

Wiener, Scott. "Food Movers: The Secret Evolution of the Pizza Box." *Food+City*, June 12, 2018.

8. THE FUTURE OF PIZZA IN COLUMBUS

"The 2019 Pizza Power Report." *PMQ Pizza Magazine*, December 2018.
   https://www.pmq.com.

Note: Luigi's information was obtained from its website in 2019. The information on the website has changed as of May 2020 and is no longer available

ABOUT THE AUTHOR

The first slice of pizza Jim Ellison had was from Dante's in Clintonville. He was four or five years old. It took a while for him to wrap his head around the concept, but by fourth grade, he was a convert. At the newly opened Clintonville Academy, there was no lunchroom or cafeteria, so Ellison and his classmates had pizza day either once per week or per month from Dante's. During the same era, Pizza Quick on English Muffins and Stouffer's French Bread pizza were trending with the middle school set. His middle and high school years involved a lot of pizza consumption at Francos, Villa Nova, Pizza House and Iaconos. College introduced Flying Pizza and Adriaticos and, eventually, post grad was Hounddogs.

In his mid-twenties, Ellison became enthralled by all things food and starting writing about it—for pay—in 1998. The first few years of the twenty-first century brought two failed book projects—one about pizza at the global level and the other about regional sandwiches around the country. He started his blog, *CMH Gourmand*, in 2006 and dabbled in podcasting and a radio show.

In the fall of 2018, Ellison was looking for a way to supplement his income. In 2013, he had started a pizza tour for his former company, Columbus Brew Adventures. This led to researching the history of Columbus pizza in much more detail. In putting the tour together, he was connected with great partners at his four featured pizzerias—Meisters, Iaconos, Late Night Slice and Hounddogs. Ellison learned a lot about their businesses, met great people and created some interesting memories. Several of his guests said, "You should write a book." The customer is always right, so this book was written.